Answering English Literature Questions
*Advice on tackling examination questions
with specimen answers*

Answering English Literature Question

**Advice on tackling examination questions
with specimen answers**

Elizabeth Gordon M.A. (Oxon) Dip. Ed.

Macmillan Education
London and Basingstoke

First published 1983

Published by
MACMILLAN EDUCATION LIMITED
Houndmills Basingstoke Hampshire RG21 2XS
and London
Associated companies in Delhi Dublin
Hong Kong Johannesburg Lagos Melbourne
New York Singapore and Tokyo

Printed in Hong Kong

First examinations

As You Like It	
A Midsummer Night's Dream	
King Henry IV Part One	William Shakespeare
Julius Caesar	
Twelfth Night	
She Stoops to Conquer	Oliver Goldssmith
Pygmalion	George Bernard Shaw
Great Expectations	Charles Dickens
'The Solitary Reaper'	William Wordsworth
'The Dead'	Rupert Brooke
'Bavarian Gentians'	D.H. Lawrence
'Felix Randell'	Gerard Manley Hopkins
'Evans'	R.S. Thomas
'Michael'	William Wordsworth
The Poems of Wilfred Owen	
Northanger Abbey	Jane Austen
'Morte d'Arthur'	Alfred, Lord Tennyson
'The Rime of the Ancient Mariner'	Samuel Taylor Coleridge

Advanced examinations

Miscellany One and *Miscellany Two*	Dylan Thomas
'Sunk Lyonesse'	Walter de la Mare
The New Men	C.P. Snow

NB I have considered it more helpful to spread the lower level questions over a number of texts but to concentrate the advanced level questions on two books only, which have thus been studied in some depth.

Preface

During my thirty-six years' experience as a GCE examiner at O and A levels, it has become abundantly clear to me that a great many candidates in English Literature are sent into the examination room with only the haziest idea, sometimes no idea at all, of what is required of them in attempting to answer the questions. This must be because the teacher either does not know or has failed to impart this knowledge to the candidates. In either case help is needed. Often far more attention seems to have been paid by the candidate to the introduction to a set book than to the text itself and, whatever questions may be asked, large undigested chunks of the introduction will appear in the answers, whether relevant (which is rare) or not.

It is obviously impossible to cover every text which has been, or might be, prescribed. A selection of frequently-set Shakespeare plays will be found here, including a history, a tragedy and some of the best-known comedies; there are also an eighteenth-century comedy, various anthologies of poetry, a Shaw play, novels by Jane Austen and Charles Dickens and another by one of our foremost contemporary writers, the late C.P. Snow. All these provide a wide range of examples and questions of every type have been answered on them. Candidates studying different plays, poems and novels should not find it too difficult to apply the techniques used in these answers, and summarized at the end of each section, to their own prescribed texts. It would be a very useful form of revision to try, for example, to give an account of a scene or two from their own plays, or to 'appreciate' a poem, closely following the methods set out in this book.

It may be that the teacher over-estimates the ability of pupils to comprehend such matters as the weighting of the different parts of a question. It is necessary to grasp whether these parts are of equal importance and likely to be equally marked or whether the first part is obviously far more demanding and thus likely to be awarded most of the total marks, while the rest of the question, which can, perhaps, be answered fully in two or three sentences, does not merit more than a few marks. To the teacher reading the question this is so evident that it may not occur to him to point out possibility in advance to his pupils. However, the less able candidates need to be taken through question after question from old papers and to be instructed in the technique of answering them. They need explanations of exactly what these questions involve, how they are to be tackled, how much illustration is expected and so on. Even the meaning of a phrase which appears year after year in questions on set plays, 'by quotation from or close reference to the text' is frequently misunderstood and whole speeches from Shakespeare's plays or dozens of lines of *Paradise Lost* are written out in full, whereas it is the candidate's ability to select just the appropriate line or two to support the point being made that is being tested. 'Close reference' to the text means just what it says, a constant pointing to the actions and words, perhaps only a single word, of the characters to substantiate the view the candidate is propounding.

It is not much good just saying that Macbeth is brave, it is necessary to prove this by describing his brave actions or quoting his brave words or telling how other people praised his bravery or doing all three. 'Quotation' demands the exact words of the text, 'close reference', the candidate's reproduction of the speech or scene in his or her own words, though keeping as near to the original as possible, so that an echo of it can be heard underlying the reproduced version. Without a good deal of practice at this sort of thing during their preparation, most candidates are not going to be able to produce spontaneously what is required when the time comes, in examinations at any level.

I do not suppose I should have ventured upon producing this book if I had not received a great many requests from teachers to do so. But I am left in no doubt that there is a crying need for authoritative guidance on the technique of answering Literature questions and many students too are now asking for this sort of help. Neither the expert, experienced teacher nor the really able candidate will, obviously, have the slightest need of such assistance as is here provided. The book is not intended for them but for teachers doubtful of their own ability because of lack of experience or a history of poor results, and for students who feel they are not getting the help they need in class.

The specimen answers given here are not those which a professor of English, or even an undergraduate, might be expected to write but those which a good candidate of 16 or 18 years old could produce. Indeed the answers have, to a large extent, been produced by pupils in schools or colleges of further education, with whom I have discussed the questions thoroughly and whose views I have accepted for purposes of this book, regardless of my own opinions. The vocabulary used is often theirs, not mine, and I have resisted the temptation to make it more scholarly. The sentence construction is sometimes clumsy but it is their own or very near to their own. Sometimes the present tense is preferred, sometimes the past.

The length of some of the answers may surprise some teachers. Careful tests have shown that they can all be written comfortably in the allotted time. They are long enough to include all the requirements of the question but not longer than that.

There are as many ways of answering a question as there are hands to write. The last thing I intend is that the answers which follow (except in the case of context questions, which are mainly factual) should be taken as models of what is correct and that, therefore, anything which differs from them is wrong.

A study of them will, however, show candidates how other students at the same age and stage have tackled the sort of Literature questions that they will, themselves, encounter. The selection of texts used here is a comparatively irrelevant matter; it is the method of dealing with the questions that is important and, once grasped, the method can be applied to answering questions on any text, whatever the students' views may be. However, in order to make answers more meaningful to candidates unfamiliar with the texts, introductory explanatory notes have been included whenever it seemed they might be helpful.

Candidates who wish to broaden their study of literature beyond the prescribed set books might well try to read for themselves some of the plays, poems and novels referred to in this book. For the Shakespeare plays I recommend the Macmillan Shakespeare edition, where straight-forward, helpful introductions and informative and easily understood notes are to be found, and many of the other texts mentioned can be obtained from the same publisher.

1 Context Questions

INTRODUCTION

Briefness and accuracy are the two qualities required in answering context questions. Many candidates have obviously been taught that they must write a complete sentence in answer to each section. This is often quite unnecessary and it is time-wasting and irritating to the examiner. It is also very important to give only the information asked for; no marks will be awarded for any irrelevant matter.

QUESTIONS FOR FIRST EXAMINATIONS

AS YOU LIKE IT

EXPLANATORY NOTE

Rosalind, an orphan, has been brought up at the court of her uncle, Duke Frederick, who has overthrown the rightful ruler, her father and his brother, Duke Senior. Celia, Duke Frederick's motherless daughter, loves Rosalind dearly and the two girls have been brought up together, like sisters. Duke Senior is living in the nearby Forest of Arden with those of his courtiers who remain loyal to him, including the melancholy Jaques.

Near to the court live the three De Boys brothers, also orphans. The eldest, Oliver, hates the next one, Orlando, and treats him worse than he would a servant, though the youngest brother, another Jaques, is being well-educated and cared for. Oliver even goes so far as to plot Orlando's murder by persuading Charles, the court wrestler, to kill him, as if accidentally, during a wrestling-match.

When he goes to the court for the match, Orlando meets Rosalind and they fall in love at first sight. Oliver's plan miscarries as Orlando overthrows Charles but, in spite of his victory, he is warned that the Duke dislikes him and may harm him. As he cannot expect any protection from Oliver, he and his father's faithful old servant, Adam, decide to escape to the Forest of Arden.

Meanwhile at court the disagreeable Duke Frederick has turned against Rosalind too, thinking that she is more popular with the people than his own daughter and, ignoring Celia's prayers, he orders her to go into banishment

1

immediately. Celia insists on accompanying her and so does the faithful court jester, Touchstone, who is later to have many arguments with the melancholy Jaques, and they steal away secretly to seek Rosalind's father in the Forest. For their safety, the girls disguise themselves as peasants, Rosalind as a boy, Ganymede, and Celia as 'his' supposed sister, Aliena.

Both Rosalind and Orlando leave with heavy hearts, wondering if they will ever see each other again but they are soon to meet in the Forest. Rosalind, of course, at once recognizes Orlando who, with Adam, has joined Duke Senior and his followers but he believes her to be the peasant boy she appears and tells 'him' the story of his lost love. Rosalind pretends to be able to cure him of his painful love-sickness and so cleverly brings it about that they meet frequently.

Rosalind and Celia make friends with some shepherds, a young man, Silvius, who is deeply in love with the scornful, unyielding Phebe, and old Corin. Phebe, believing Rosalind to be a boy, falls in love with 'him'.

Meanwhile Duke Frederick has sent Oliver to find and bring back Rosalind and Celia, under threat of death if he is unsuccessful. He is nearly killed by a lion in the Forest but is rescued just in time by Orlando and consequently has a complete change of heart and becomes a loving brother to Orlando and, eventually, Celia's bridegroom.

Phebe in due course discovers Rosalind's true sex and so consents to marry Silvius, and Orlando finds out who Rosalind really is and marries her. Duke Frederick, like Oliver, repents of all his previous wickedness and restores the dukedom to Duke Senior, now re-united with his daughter, so everything ends happily.

Context (a) shows Celia pleading with her father not to banish Rosalind.

(b) is part of a description of Touchstone given by the melancholy Jaques to Duke Senior.

In (c) Orlando is asking Rosalind for the cure for his love-sickness which she pretends her uncle, a magician, taught her.

(d) is Rosalind's advice to Phebe to accept Silvius's proposal.

QUESTION

Choose three of the following passages (a) — (d) and answer briefly the questions which follow.

(a)   I did not then entreat to have her stay;
It was your pleasure and your own remorse
I was too young that time to value her;
But now I know her; if she be a traitor,
Why so am I.

    (i)   Who is speaking and to whom? Who is the 'traitor'?
    (ii)   Explain: 'It was your pleasure and your own remorse'.
    (iii) How does the person addressed justify his action?
    (iv) Briefly refer to another instance of his tyranny.

(b)   And then he drew a dial from his poke,
And, looking, on it with lack-lustre eye,
Says very wisely, 'It is ten o'clock;
Thus may we see,' quoth he, 'how the world wags'.

    (i)   Who is speaking? Whom is he describing?
    (ii)   In your own words conclude this little sermon on Time.
    (iii)   What ambition is awakened in the speaker as a result of this meeting in the forest?
    (iv)   How does Duke Senior express his disapproval of this ambition?

(c)   Orlando. 'I am he that is so loved-shaked. I pray you, tell me your remedy.'
Rosalind. 'There is none of my uncle's marks upon you: he taught me how to know a man in love; in which cage of rushes I am sure you are not prisoner.'

    (i)   Explain the reference to 'my uncle'.
    (ii)   Instance *three* of the marks of a lover as Rosalind goes on to describe them.
    (iii)   What is her remedy for love?
    (iv)   Explain 'cage of rushes'.

(d)   But, mistress, know yourself; down on your knees,
And thank heaven, fasting, for a good man's love;
For I must tell you friendly in your ear
Sell when you can; you are not for all markets.

    (i)   Who is speaking and to whom?
    (ii)   Who is the 'good man' and how, according to the speaker, does he show his love? How has his love been received?
    (iii)   Explain the last line.
    (iv)   What is the effect of this speech upon the person to whom it is addressed?

ANSWER

(a)   (i)   Celia is speaking to her father, Duke Frederick. The 'traitor' is Rosalind.
       (ii)   You allowed her to stay of your own free will from a feeling of compassion.
       (iii)   He tells Celia that Rosalind is cleverly deceiving her and by her uncomplaining submission is appealing to the people who feel sorry for her and esteem her more than

they do the Duke's own daughter. When Celia has no longer to compete with Rosalind, her good qualities will be more easily recognized.

(iv) When the Duke discovers that Orlando is missing he sends for Oliver, who has no knowledge of his brother's whereabouts, and tells him that unless he produces Orlando, alive or dead, within a year, he will be exiled and all his possessions confiscated.

(b) (i) Jaques is describing Touchstone.

(ii) An hour ago it was nine o'clock and in another hour's time it will be eleven. So, as the hours pass, we come to maturity and then begin to decline.
There is more that could be said on this subject.

(iii) To become a jester.

(iv) By telling Jaques that he would do wrong to find fault with others for, having been a dissolute sinner himself, he might well as a result of his former evil life, corrupt rather than reform.

(c) (i) Rosalind has explained her refined accent to Orlando by telling him that an old rebellious uncle of hers taught her to speak.

(ii) 'A lean cheek', a 'blue eye and sunken', 'a beard neglected'.

(iii) She suggests to Orlando that he should pretend that she was his beloved and should come every day to court her. She would then behave in such a maddeningly inconsistent way towards him that he should become sickened by her moods and vagaries and would wish to find refuge in retirement in some secluded place.

(iv) Rosalind is likening a man in love to a caged bird which has lost its freedom. A bird cage in Shakespeare's time would be made of basket-work, interwoven rushes or osiers.

(d) (i) Rosalind is speaking to Phebe.

(ii) Silvius is the good man, who follows Phebe, 'like foggy south puffing with wind and rain' and flatters her into having far too high an opinion of herself. Phebe has rejected his love cruelly and insultingly, showing her proud and ruthless disposition.

(iii) Marry while you have the opportunity, it is not everyone who would be likely to make you an offer.

(iv) Phebe falls in love with the disguised Rosalind and tells her she would rather listen to her scolding than to Silvius's protestations of love.

NB All four parts of the question have been answered here, although only three are asked for in the question.

A MIDSUMMER NIGHT'S DREAM

EXPLANATORY NOTE

There are three threads in the complicated plot of this play, which is set in Athens in ancient times. The Duke, Theseus, is about to be married to Queen Hippolyta and some rough working-men, led by Nick Bottom, a weaver, are preparing a play which they hope will be chosen to be acted before the wedding-guests. In order to keep their plans secret, they rehearse at night in the forest outside Athens.

This forest is the home of fairies, whose King and Queen, Oberon and Titania, are quarrelling bitterly over a little Indian boy adopted by Titania, who is, in Oberon's view, occupying far too much of her time and attention. He devises a plan to put matters right and sends his mischievous little servant, Puck, to fetch a flower, the juice of which has magic properties. He proposes to smear the juice on the sleeping Titania's eyes. This will cause her to fall in love with the first creature she sees when she awakes. Oberon will then at once kidnap the Indian boy and after that take the spell off Titania with some different juice, so that she will once more love her husband whole-heartedly.

Puck chances upon Bottom and his friends rehearsing their play and, seizing a moment when Bottom is alone, he pops a sort of donkey-mask over his head. Bottom doesn't know quite what has happened to him and his friends are terrified at his changed appearance and run away, screaming. Blundering about in the darkness, the bewildered Bottom wakes Titania who immediately adores him. Oberon takes away the Indian boy and then frees Titania from the spell as planned, so that she loves him again and loathes the sight of poor Bottom who, after Puck has taken off his ass's head, makes his way back to his friends, just in time for the choosing of the play for the wedding entertainment.

Besides all this excitement going on in the forest, four young Athenian lovers are also out there that night. Hermia and Lysander are eloping because Hermia's father, Egeus, won't let them be married; Demetrius, who is favoured by Egeus, is pursuing them in the hope of marrying Hermia himself and Helena, who loves Demetrius, is tagging along behind on the chance of being thrown a kind word by Demetrius. Oberon tries to make all four happy by using his magic juice to cause Demetrius to stop loving Hermia and love Helena instead, but Puck puts the juice on Lysander's eyes by mistake and great complications result from this till, at last, Oberon is able to put things right and the play ends with the wedding, not only of Duke Theseus and Queen Hippolyta but also of Lysander and Hermia and Demetrius and Helena.

Bottom's entertainment is, of course, chosen to be performed at the party afterwards. This play is the harrowing story of a young lover, Pyramus and his beloved, Thisbe, who have to meet in secret by night because of Thisbe's father's objection to their marriage. Thisbe arrives first at their meeting-place but is frightened away by a lion, dropping her cloak as she runs off. The lion chews the cloak with blood-stained jaws, so that when Pyramus arrives and finds it, he believes Thisbe has been eaten by the lion and, overcome with grief, kills himself. Thisbe then bravely returns and, seeing her lover lying dead, stabs herself to death with his sword. Bottom plays the part of Pyramus and, of course, the play should produce an effect both thrilling and sorrowful but, as acted by Bottom and his friends, the only sort of tears it is likely to cause are tears of laughter.

In context (a) Helena is thinking aloud about the mysteries of love and the reason for Demetrius's preferring Hermia to her.

(b) is part of Puck's description to the fairy King Oberon of the terrified flight of Bottom's friends when they first see him wearing the ass's head and tells how, for fun, he deliberately added to their bewilderment and fear.

In (c) Theseus is telling his bride that he cannot accept as the truth the four lovers' hazy recollections of what happened to them the previous night in the forest.

(d) is also Theseus talking to Hippolyta, this time about his choice of play for their wedding entertainment. She expects to be bored by the efforts of Bottom and his friends and he is explaining why he has selected their play from all the others offered.

QUESTION

Choose three of the passages (a) — (d) and answer briefly the questions that follow them:

(a) *Helena* Things base and vile, holding no quantity
Love can transpose to form and dignity;
Love looks not with the eyes but with the mind,
And therefore is wing'd Cupid painted blind.
Nor hath love's mind of any judgment taste;
Wings and no eyes figure unheedy haste;
And therefore is Love said to be a child,
Because in choice he is so oft beguil'd.

   (i) State what happens immediately before this speech.
   (ii) Give the meaning in this passage of 'figure' and 'beguil'd'.
   (iii) Put line 5 into your own words.
   (iv) What light does this passage throw upon the character of the speaker?

(b)
> So, at this sight, away his fellows fly,
> And, at our stamp, here o'er and o'er one falls;
> He murder cries, and help from Athens calls.
> Their sense thus weak, lost with their fears thus strong,
> Made senseless things begin to do them wrong;
> For briers and thorns at their apparel snatch;
> Some sleeves, some hats, from yielders all things catch.
> I led them on in this distracted fear,
> And left sweet Pyramus translated there.

(i) Who is the speaker and to whom is the speech addressed?
(ii) State what happened immediately after this speech.
(iii) Give the meaning in this passage of 'from yielders all things catch'.
(iv) Express in your own words the meaning of line 4.
(v) In what way had Bottom been 'translated'?

(c) *Theseus* More strange than true. I never may believe
> These antique fables, nor these fairy toys.
> Lovers and madmen have such seething brains
> Such shaping fantasies, that apprehend
> More than cool reason ever comprehends.
> The lunatic, the lover, and the poet,
> Are of imagination all compact.

(i) To whom is the speech addressed?
(ii) State what happens immediately before this speech.
(iii) Give the meaning of 'fairy toys' and 'compact'.
(iv) Put lines 4 and 5 into your own words.
(v) Say briefly what choice Theseus has to make soon after he says these words, and what decision he comes to.

(d)
> Trust me, sweet,
> Out of this silence yet I picked a welcome
> And in the modesty of fearful duty
> I read as much as from the rattling tongue
> Of saucy and audacious eloquence.
> Love, therefore, and tongue-tied simplicity
> In least speak most, to my capacity.

(i) Who is the speaker and to whom is the speech addressed?
(ii) State what happens immediately before this speech.
(iii) Give the meaning of 'in the modesty of fearful duty'.
(iv) Express in your own words what is meant by line 7.

7

(v)   What light does the whole passage throw upon the character of the speaker?

ANSWER

(a)   (i)   Hermia and Lysander have told Helena of their secret intention to run away from Athens together on the following night because of the refusal of Egeus, Hermia's father, to allow their marriage.

(ii) 'Figure' means 'symbolise' or 'represent', 'beguil'd' means 'tricked'.

(iii) Nor has Cupid's brain any ability to discriminate.

(iv) We see here Helena's romantic nature and her vanity in assuming that, if Cupid were more discriminating, she would be preferred to Hermia by Demetrius.

(b)   (i)   Puck is speaking to Oberon.

(ii) Demetrius and Hermia entered. He was pleading for her love and she was bitterly rejecting him and accusing him of killing Lysander.

(iii) Everything is readily given up (by those who are too frightened to safeguard their possessions).

(iv) The extremity of their terror causes them to lose their heads completely.

(v)   Puck has disguised him by placing an ass's head over his own.

(c)   (i)   Hippolyta.

(ii) Hippolyta has commented on the mysterious nature of the account the four Athenian lovers have given of their experiences in the forest.

(iii) 'Fairy toys' means 'fanciful stories about fairies' and 'compact' means 'composed'.

(iv) Such imaginative powers capable of giving shape to things that have no real existence, which conjure up more than can ever be grasped by the exercise of sober rational thought.

(v)   Theseus has to choose one of the four possible entertainments selected by Philostrate to be performed at the Wedding Feast. He chooses 'A tedious brief scene of young Pyramus and his love Thisbe; very tragical mirth' offered by Bottom and the other 'Mechanicals'.

(d)   (i)   Theseus is speaking to Hippolyta.

8

(ii) Hippolyta has expressed her disapproval of Theseus's choice of play for their wedding entertainment, fearing that the actors have been over-ambitious and will be embarrassingly unable to do justice to their theme.

(iii) In the timid attempt offered in all humility to do what was required.

(iv) The less articulate they are, the more they manage to convey in my opinion.

(v) We see here Theseus's tolerance and sensitive perception.

NB All four parts of the question have been answered here, although only three are asked for in the question.

KING HENRY IV PART ONE

EXPLANATORY NOTE

This play deals with the relationship of King Henry IV with his eldest son, the heir to the throne, Prince Hal, against a background of rebellious lords, who hope to depose Henry, whose right to the throne they dispute because he, himself, seized it from his cousin, Richard II. One of these rebels, Northumberland, has a son, Hotspur, who is brave, honourable and loyally supportive of his father, whereas Prince Hal leads a lazy, self-indulgent life, drinking in the company of his good-for-nothing friends, chief of whom is Sir John Falstaff, a fat, degenerate knight who is, in spite of his failings, one of Shakespeare's greatest humorous characters.

In the course of the play the young Prince reforms surprisingly, casts off his old friends and fights nobly for his father against the rebels at the battle of Shrewsbury, killing Hotspur in a hand-to-hand duel.

In context (a) The King is reflecting sadly on the apparent superiority of Northumberland's son, Hotspur, to his own son, Hal.

(b) is part of Falstaff's conversation with the Prince in the course of which they plan a highway robbery.

In (c) Hotspur is teasing his spirited young wife, Kate, who is trying to find out what has been occupying his mind so greatly in the last couple of weeks. Believing that the only secret she is capable of keeping is the secret she doesn't know, he refuses to tell her about the planned rebellion.

(d) is taken from a discussion about future policy in which various members of the rebels' party express their opinions. Glendower, who is the 'worthy gentleman' mentioned, is a Welsh supporter, endowed, at any rate in his own view, with strange, supernatural powers.

QUESTION

Choose **three** of the following passages (a) — (d) and answer briefly the questions which follow them.

(a) Yea, there thou mak'st me sad and mak'st me sin
In envy that my Lord Northumberland
Should be the father to so blest a son,
A son who is the theme of honour's tongue;
Amongst a grove the very straightest plant;
Who is sweet Fortune's minion and her pride.

(i) Name the speaker.
(ii) Name the person or persons addressed.
(iii) Describe very briefly the immediate circumstances in which the words were spoken.
(iv) Explain 'the theme of honour's tongue'.

(b) Let not us that are squires of the night's body be called thieves of the day's beauty; let us be Diana's foresters, gentlemen of the shade, minions of the moon; and let men say, we be men of good government, being governed as the sea is, by our noble and chaste mistress the moon, under whose countenance we steal.

(i) Name the speaker.
(ii) Name the person or persons addressed.
(iii) Describe very briefly the immediate circumstances in which the words were spoken.
(iv) Explain 'let us be Diana's foresters, gentlemen of the shade, minions of the moon'.

(c) Constant you are,
But yet a woman; and for secrecy
No lady closer; for I well believe
Thou wilt not utter what thou dost not know;
And so far will I trust thee.

(i) Name the speaker.
(ii) Name the person or persons addressed.
(iii) Describe very briefly the immediate circumstances in which the words were spoken.
(iv) How far does the extract suggest that the speaker's trust will go?

(d) In faith, he is a worthy gentleman,
Exceedingly well read, and profited
In strange concealments, valiant as a lion
And wondrous affable, and as bountiful
As mines of India.

(i) Name the speaker.
(ii) Name the person or persons addressed.
(iii) Describe very briefly the immediate circumstances in which the words were spoken.
(iv) Explain 'profited in strange concealments' and 'as bountiful As mines of India'.

ANSWER

(a) (i) King Henry IV.
    (ii) Earl of Westmoreland.
    (iii) Rebellions against the King had broken out, led by those who disputed his claim to the throne which he had taken from his cousin, Richard II. Lord Northumberland's son, Henry Hotspur, had distinguished himself fighting against Scottish rebels and had taken prisoner many of the leaders.
    (iv) The man sure to be mentioned in every conversation about heroism on the battlefield.

(b) (i) Falstaff.
    (ii) The Prince of Wales.
    (iii) The Prince and Falstaff were joking together companionably in the Prince's apartment.
    (iv) All these phrases mean 'men who go out at night'.
    Diana was the huntress Goddess of the moon, so her attendants might well move by night. The 'shade' refers to the darkness of night. 'Minions' is here used as 'servants'.

(c) (i) Hotspur, Henry Percy.
    (ii) His wife Kate, Lady Percy.
    (iii) Kate was trying to discover why her husband had been so pre-occupied for the last fortnight and whether he was planning to join an insurrection in support of her brother Mortimer's claim to the throne. Hotspur teasingly refused to answer her questions or tell her where he was going.
    (iv) He did not trust her at all. He believed the only secrets which she would not betray were those of which she was in ignorance.

(d) (i) Edmund Mortimer.
    (ii) Hotspur and Worcester.

(iii) Mortimer, Hotspur and Worcester had been in conference with Glendower at the Archdeacon of Bangor's house to examine the Archdeacon's division of England and Wales into three parts, to be governed by Mortimer, Hotspur, and Glendower respectively, once the King should have been defeated by their forces. After Glendower had left the room, Hotspur criticized him for his boring talk about his supernatural powers and Mortimer spoke these words in Glendower's defence.

(iv) 'Proficient in mysterious secrets' and 'as rich and ready to pour forth his wealth as India her treasures'.

NB All four parts of the question have been answered here, although only three are asked for in the question.

SUMMING-UP

The introduction to this section stated the necessity for briefness and accuracy and these answers will have shown you how these two qualities may be achieved. You will have seen that a short paraphrase is often asked for, as in (a)ii and (d)iii. It is very important, when you substitute your own for the given words, that you reproduce the exact meaning of the original, neither adding nor omitting anything at all. You will also have noticed that you may be asked to refer to something or somebody in a quite different part of the play, as in (a)iv for example, so that a context question is, in fact, much wider than it may seem and involves a great deal more than merely knowing where the given lines occur in the course of the play or poem.

2 Questions Requiring Accounts of Scenes

INTRODUCTION

Such questions are very common and are straightforward memory tests. Almost invariably there is a second part of the question which demands something more difficult, usually comment on character.

Some candidates who attempt such questions have only the vaguest knowledge of the scene and produce one or two imprecise recollections, possibly in the wrong order. The best candidates, on the other hand, will know the scene quite or almost by heart. Some of these hard workers sometimes make the mistake of writing the whole scene out from memory and no doubt congratulate themselves on having done extremely well. Unfortunately this is not what 'Give an account . . .' means. Certainly a detailed knowledge of the scene is necessary to start off with but the test lies in the candidates' skill in reproducing the events in their own words, high-lighting the important points, suggesting the emotions of the speakers by the selective use of vocabulary and generally bringing the whole thing to life. The born story-teller has a great advantage in this type of question but every candidate can be helped to reach a passable standard. Long quotations are not required but short ones, consisting of a line or two, or less, are essential and must be worked into the account as often and as naturally as possible.

As far as the second part of the question is concerned, a candidate should, of course, have a thorough knowledge of all the principal characters in the set play and if, as is generally the case, the candidate is asked to show what light the scene throws on one or more of these characters, there should be no difficulty in deciding which of his, or their qualities are most clearly in evidence. It is not enough to list a number of characteristics; each one mentioned must be supported, either by quoting from or referring closely to the text. If, for example, the candidate states that someone shows selfishness in the scene, then either the selfish words must be quoted, or the selfish action described. Then the point is made and deserves marks — without this corroboration, guess-work might often be too generously rewarded.

JULIUS CAESAR

EXPLANATORY NOTE

The play of *Julius Caesar* deals at first with the planning of the assassination of Caesar by a group of conspirators, only one of whom, Marcus Brutus, is spurred on by disinterested and patriotic motives. Realizing Caesar's growing ambition for power, he fears that he will make himself a dictator, thus threatening the freedom of his fellow Romans. The other conspirators are Cassius, Casca, Trebonius, Ligarius, Decius, Metellus Cimber and Cinna.

The second part of the play, after the assassination has taken place, tells how Caesar's friend, Mark Antony, devotes himself to taking revenge on Brutus and his allies, defeating them finally at the battle of Philippi.

The meeting of the conspirators in Brutus's orchard happens in the first scene of the second act. Lucius is a young boy, a servant to Brutus.

The murder of Caesar comes in Act III Scene I. The Soothsayer, or fore-teller of the future (literally 'one who speaks the truth'), makes a second attempt here to warn Caesar of his coming fate. The Ides of March is the Roman way of giving the date, 15 March, and 'Et tu, Brute' means 'And you, too Brutus!', an expression of Caesar's shocked and sad incredulity that the friend he had loved, trusted and esteemed had joined with his enemies in the murder-plot against him.

Later in this book, in the section on character studies, there is a question on Portia, the wife of Brutus, Cassius, his chief fellow-conspirator, and Antony and Octavius, who is Julius Caesar's great-nephew and adopted son. Octavius fights with Mark Antony at the battle of Philippi and helps to defeat the conspirators. (In Shakespeare's later play, *Antony and Cleopatra*, we see the rivalry which develops between these two great leaders, becoming a personal hatred which ends only with the death of Antony, leaving Octavius triumphant.)

This question does not demand complete character-sketches and, although we do not learn elsewhere much more about Portia than we can gather from the scene prescribed, the greatness of both Cassius and Antony is not fully brought out in the episodes asked for here.

QUESTION

Tell, so as to bring out its dramatic qualities, the story of the scene in the Capitol from Caesar's encounter with the Soothsayer to the murder. What light do Caesar's remarks in this scene throw on his character?

ANSWER

'The essence of drama is conflict'. In this scene there is, of course, a tremendous conflict between the conspirators and Caesar whom they actually murder and this conflict is underlying almost every speech that is uttered in the scene, making it one of the most dramatic scenes in the play.

As Caesar makes his way to take his place in the Senate House, the same Soothsayer who has earlier warned him to 'beware the Ides of March', now pushes himself forward to warn him again. Caesar, seeing him, remarks confidently 'The Ides of March are come' but the Soothsayer, in ominous tones, reminds him, 'Ay, Caesar, but not gone'.

Next Artemidorus thrusts himself forward and implores Caesar to read 'this Schedule', the warning he has written out for him. Decius tries to stop Caesar from reading it by telling him Trebonius has a more urgent petition. Artemidorus tells Caesar his suit 'touches Caesar nearer' but Caesar passes on, saying that anything concerning him personally will be the last matter he will attend to, and, in any case, the Senate House is the proper place to present petitions.

As Caesar takes his place, Popilius Lena whispers to Cassius 'I wish your enterprise today may thrive'. Cassius repeats this to Brutus and, for an intensely suspenseful moment, the two conspirators watch Popilius as he goes up to Caesar and whispers in his ear. They hardly dare breathe and Cassius even says 'I will slay myself' if their plan is discovered, but all is well for they see that 'Caesar doth not change'.

Trebonius next carries out his part of the conspiracy by making some excuse to draw 'Mark Antony out of the way'.

Now the final stage of the plan to murder Caesar begins and Metellus Cimber moves forward to present his suit for the repeal of his brother, Publius Cimber, from banishment, while the other conspirators crowd behind him. Metellus kneels down and begins a speech to Caesar but Caesar tells him to stand up, as he hates such 'couchings' and 'lowly courtesies' and 'base spaniel-fawning'. He tells Metellus his brother has been legally banished by decree of the court and he will not listen to any pleas for him. Metellus turns round and asks for support and Brutus kisses Caesar's hand and, to Caesar's astonishment, echoes Metellus's request. Cassius next throws himself down at Caesar's feet and begs 'enfranchisement for Publius Cimber'. Caesar declares that, although an ordinary man might easily be moved by all their prayers, he is 'constant as the northern star' and is determined that Cimber shall remain in banishment. Cinna and Decius cry to Caesar but Casca goes further and shouting 'Speak, hands, for me!' he plunges his dagger into Caesar, closely followed by all the other conspirators, with Brutus a reluctant last.

Until Brutus stabs, Caesar has gallantly remained on his feet. When he sees his trusted friend striking at him he utters his final words 'Et, tu, Brute! Then fall, Caesar!' and sinks lifeless to the ground.

The conspirators then rush about the streets, proclaiming the end of Caesar's tyranny and the birth of a new age of liberty.

Various aspects of Caesar's character are revealed in this scene. We see his greatness and nobility when he refuses to attend to any matter concerning himself personally until everybody else's affairs have been settled. He speaks of his dislike of flattery and says he cannot bear to have suitors kneeling before him but here he is wrong in his estimate of himself, for Decius has said in the scene in Brutus's orchard that Caesar is very susceptible to flattery and we have already seen Decius persuade Caesar, by means of flattery, to go to the Senate House after he has promised Calphurnia to stay at home.

He has a very high opinion of himself and we cannot help thinking some of his utterances seem very conceited, e.g. 'Know, Caesar doth not wrong', and also his declaration that he is the only man in the world who steadfastly pursues his course, no matter who is trying to divert him.

He seems to be very strong-willed, saying 'I am constant as the northern star', but we have seen him not at all able to stick to his decision to remain at home in the face of Decius's flattery.

The last aspect of Caesar's character we see in this scene is his undoubted courage. He faces his enemies on his feet and without a cry, although he must have been suffering agony and the last impression of him that we take away with us is of his gallantry.

QUESTION

Give an account of the meeting of the conspirators at the house of Brutus. How does this episode reveal the strength and weakness of Brutus?

ANSWER

After Brutus has decided in his own mind that Caesar must die, not because he is at the moment dangerous to Rome, but because like 'the serpent's egg', he may become so, Lucius comes out into the orchard to bring him a letter, supposedly from a Roman citizen, urging him to 'Speak! Strike! Redress!' It is 14 March and Lucius next informs his master that Cassius and others, muffled up to avoid recognition, are waiting to come in. While they are being admitted Brutus shows his dislike of the need for concealment.

Cassius presents all the conspirators, Casca, Decius, Cinna, Metellus Cimber and Trebonius to Brutus who shakes hands with them all. Cassius wants them all to swear an oath of secrecy about their conspiracy but Brutus, believing that a Roman's word alone is sufficient, will not have this. Cassius next suggests that Cicero should be asked to join the conspiracy because he is such a good orator but Brutus will not have this either because he says Cicero will 'never follow anything that other men begin'. Cassius's next proposal is that Antony shall be killed with Caesar so that that 'shrewd contriver' will not be able to ruin their plans. Brutus is shocked at this suggestion and says that if they could kill Caesar's spirit without killing Caesar's body, they certainly would. 'Let us be sacrificers but not butchers'. Furthermore he confidently declares that Antony 'can do no more than Caesar's arm, when Caesar's head is off'.

Cassius is afraid that Caesar who is 'superstitious grown of late' may not attend the Senate the next day because of all the 'apparent prodigies', which have recently been seen in Rome. Decius declares that he can deal with this problem by flattering Caesar and they all arrange to call for Caesar 'at the eighth hour'.

Finally Metellus proposes that Caius Ligarius shall be included in the conspiracy and Brutus asks Metellus to approach him, after which all the conspirators depart leaving Brutus alone.

This scene reveals both the strength and weakness of Brutus. We see his strength in various ways. He hates everything underhand and likes things to be open and straightforward and so he detests the conspirators' disguise. He believes everyone to be as honourable as himself and so he will not agree to their swearing of an oath. This decision might have proved fatal to their plans. Somebody must have talked, because Artemidorus knew and Popilius Lena also obviously knew of their intentions when he said to Cassius just before the assassination, 'I wish your enterprise today may thrive' and he had ample opportunity to warn Caesar if he had wished to do so. Brutus hates unnecessary bloodshed and regrets the necessity to kill even Caesar. The most obvious indication of his strength in this scene is the fact that, in every case, all the conspirators give way to him and accept what he wants.

But Brutus's weaknesses are also revealed here. He is no judge of character and is completely wrong in his estimate of Antony, just as he is wrong in believing that an oath of silence is not necessary. He is over-confident, too, in their own abilities and is mistaken in thinking that they do not need Cicero's power of oratory. This is made very clear at Caesar's funeral when Antony, who is a marvellous speaker, is able to sway the crowd to follow him, and Brutus's list of reasons for killing Caesar is quite forgotten by the frenzied people whose emotions have been so powerfully stirred by Antony.

TWELFTH NIGHT

EXPLANATORY NOTE

Olivia, a rich Countess, beloved by Duke Orsino, has vowed to mourn for seven years for her brother's death. Living at her home is her disreputable and drunken old uncle, Sir Toby Belch, who spends most of his time with her servants and with his dim-witted friend, Sir Andrew Aguecheek, whom he hopes to persuade his niece to marry. Malvolio is Olivia's steward, or butler, who is in charge of her domestic arrangements and who is detested by Sir Toby and his followers for his self-importance and overbearing behaviour towards them.

They plan to take revenge on him by writing a letter, purporting to come from Olivia, which will convince Malvolio that his mistress is in love with him and thus encourage him to behave in a way so obnoxious to Olivia that she will inevitably dismiss him from her service.

This note covers only one of the themes in *Twelfth Night* and omits any mention of Viola, the true heroine of the play, and her twin brother, Sebastian, and the many adventures that befall them both before, at the end of the play, Olivia becomes the bride of Sebastian and Viola marries Duke Orsino.

QUESTION

Give an account of the scene in which Malvolio finds the letter, bringing out the humour of the situation as fully as you can.

ANSWER

This scene takes place in Olivia's garden. Her uncle, Sir Toby Belch, her suitor, Sir Andrew Aguecheek, and Fabian, one of her servants, are talking about her steward, Malvolio, 'the niggardly, rascally sheep-biter', against whom they all bear a grudge, and wishing they could somehow shame him in his mistress's eyes and 'fool him black and blue'.

They are joined by Maria, Olivia's sharp-witted maid or companion, who tells them to hide quickly in 'the box tree' as Malvolio is approaching, posturing ridiculously, and she intends to drop on the path the letter she has written, so that he cannot avoid seeing it. This is part of their plan for revenge on the hated and conceited Malvolio, who will believe that the letter comes from his mistress, Olivia, and will be encouraged by it to make such a fool of himself in his behaviour towards her that she will be enraged and dismiss him.

The three men dive into the bushes, Maria throws down the letter and runs away, and 'the trout that must be caught with tickling' advances upon his fate.

As Malvolio appears, he is soliloquizing on Olivia's attitude towards him, saying that Maria has told him Olivia fancies him and he has noticed she treats him with more respect than 'anyone else that follows her'.

The hidden watchers are furious at what they hear and utter violent threats under their breath.

Malvolio continues with his phantasizing, imagining himself with the title of Count and reminding himself of another servant who had married his mistress, while more and more angry mutterings come from the eavesdroppers.

Malvolio next considers how he will behave after 'having been three months married to her, sitting in my state'. Having come from 'a daybed', where he has 'left Olivia sleeping', and dressed in his 'branched velvet gown', he will summon his officials and servants to discuss business matters and to ensure that they know their places as surely as he knows his. He will then 'ask for my kinsman Toby'. At this last impertinence the listeners, particularly Sir Toby himself, nearly explode with rage and Sir Toby asks 'Shall this fellow live?'

He is calmed by Fabian and Malvolio proceeds with his imaginary interview with Sir Toby. He will extend his hand to him, not smiling pleasantly but 'with an austere regard of control', and will tell him that, since he is now, by his marriage to Olivia, in a position to reprimand him, he is obliged to take him to task for his drunkenness.

Again there is an outburst of smothered abuse from behind the bushes but Fabian reminds Sir Toby 'Nay, patience, or we break the sinews of our plot' and Malvolio goes on with his flattering day-dream, turning his attention to another failing of Sir Toby's, his time-wasting in the company of 'a foolish knight'. Sir Andrew is not quite so foolish as to fail to recognize himself in this description.

At last Malvolio notices Maria's letter and, scrutinizing the hand-writing on the cover, is sure that it comes from Olivia, particularly as it is sealed with her own seal, 'her Lucrece'. He

reads it aloud, pausing frequently to comment on it and inter-
preting all its cryptic phrases as signifying Olivia's passion for him.
'M, O, A, I, doth sway my life' is baffling but he is determined to
make these letters stand for 'Malvolio', 'for everyone of those
letters is in my name'. 'I may command where I adore' is easier for
of course his mistress can give him orders. The letter goes on to
tell him 'be not afraid of greatness', 'cast thy humble slough',
'be opposite with a kinsman', (obviously Sir Toby) 'surly with
servants' (such as Maria and Fabian) and to converse on 'matters
of state'. It concludes by giving him instructions about how to
dress himself in yellow stockings with cross-garters (most incongruous with his sober steward's dress) and by assuring him that
'thou art made, if thou desirest to be so'.

Malvolio is overwhelmed with joy and satisfaction and vows to
obey all the letter's suggestions. Then he finds a postscript advising
him, 'if thou entertainest my love', to smile constantly, to which
he replies aloud, 'I will smile; I will do everything that thou wilt
have me'.

He goes on his way and the delighted observers can at last give
vent to their feelings. They are triumphant at the success of their
plan and both knights declare they could marry Maria 'for this
device'. She, herself, then enters, longing to hear how the plan
worked out and she leads the others off to watch Malvolio's
meeting with Olivia, when he will doubtless be incongruously
attired in yellow stockings and cross-gartered, which she will
detest, and everlastingly smiling at her, which, in her 'melancholy'
state, will strike her very disagreeably.

The humour in this scene is so apparent that it hardly needs
underlining. Malvolio's ridiculous conceit and vanity, even before
he finds the letter, are laughable and, as the words he reads give
him encouragement to believe wholeheartedly in Olivia's love for
him his complacency becomes increasingly ludicrous. The fact
that the audience can see the furious, though necessarily smothered, reactions of the hidden listeners, particularly when Malvolio
is talking of his intended treatment of Sir Toby, adds greatly to
the fun, and the scene ends with the promise of more laughter to
come, when the comically dressed steward appears before his
bereaved mistress, with a foolish grin stretching from ear to ear.

SHE STOOPS TO CONQUER

EXPLANATORY NOTE

This eighteenth-century comedy introduces us to an elderly and old-fashioned couple, Mr and Mrs Hardcastle, who had each had a child by a previous marriage when they met and married. Mr Hardcastle's daughter is the delightful Kate, who is the 'She' of the title, and Mrs Hardcastle's son is a country bumpkin, perhaps not so stupid as he likes to pretend, whose name, Tony Lumpkin, suggests his boorish disposition.

Mr Hardcastle has an old friend, Sir Charles Marlow, whose son is still a bachelor and the two old fathers agree that it would be ideal if their children would marry each other.

Through Tony's mischievous interference, Young Marlow and his friend Hastings arrive at the Hardcastle's house, where they have been invited to stay, believing it to be an inn. The confusion and bewilderment which follow from this misapprehension give the play its sub-title, *The Mistakes of a Night*.

Young Marlow treats the Hardcastle family as his servants, which infuriates them. Kate is, however, told by her maid of her step-brother's joke and, since she is attracted to Marlow and realizes he feels a growing affection for her, she 'stoops to conquer' him by pretending to be first the barmaid of the 'inn' and, later, when Marlow, to his great embarrassment, has discovered the true situation, a poor relation of the family.

Sir Charles Marlow follows his son to his old friend's home and is told by him, truthfully as far as he understands the situation, that he has up till then hardly exchanged a word with the daughter of the house, whereas Kate assures Sir Charles and her father that the young man has talked to her on several occasions and even declared his love for her.

The interview mentioned in the question takes place at Kate's suggestion. Knowing that both their fathers are hiding, listening to her conversation with her suitor, she cleverly leads him on to protest his affection for her and it is only when the two old men rush out from behind their screen that he at last realizes who the enchanting Kate really is.

QUESTION

Describe the interview which takes place between Kate Hardcastle and young Marlow at the end of the play *She Stoops to Conquer*, and explain what led their fathers to listen. What does this episode add to your impressions of Kate?

ANSWER

Marlow, having been thrown into fearful confusion by discovering the mistake he has made in believing Mr Hardcastle's house to be an inn, has decided to leave immediately but cannot bear to go until he has bid another farewell to Kate, whom he now believes to be a poor relation to the family who is given her keep in return for her help in the house. He tells her he feels 'pain in the separation'. In her normal voice (no longer acting the barmaid) she asks him, if that is so, why he does not stay longer.

Marlow tells her that all his reasons for not marrying a poor relation of the Hardcastles are being melted away by his love. These reasons are his pride, the difference in their 'education and fortune', his father's anger and his friends' contempt at such a match. The only thing which can save him from proposing to her is to go at once. Kate tells him scornfully to go. She says money must be his first requirement in a wife, as her family and education are as good as Kate's.

The two fathers now creep in and hide behind a screen.

Marlow indignantly denies that he is after money and says it is her beauty that first attracted him and that now seems to have taken on a new refinement. He now sees in her 'courageous innocence and conscious virtue'.

After some whispering between the old fathers, unheard by the lovers, Marlow declares he is determined to stay and feels sure his father will be sensible enough to approve. Kate is unwilling to take advantage of 'a transient passion' and could not enjoy happiness with him if he later regretted their marriage. Marlow insists upon staying and is determined to woo her in respectful fashion. Kate still will not listen, saying she does not wish to appear 'mercenary', nor to see him criticized for rashness. Marlow kneels at her feet, assuring her of his devotion when, unable to bear it any longer, Sir Charles bursts out from behind the screen, closely followed by Mr Hardcastle.

Marlow has told Mr Hardcastle, in his father's presence, that 'nothing has passed' between him and Kate. He says that they have had 'but one interview', in which he 'saw the lady without emotion and parted without reluctance'. Kate, on the other hand, has told a very different story. She says that Marlow has expressed his love for her, at several interviews, and has behaved 'as most professed admirers do'. In order to find out which of these two stories is true, for each old man believes his own child, the two fathers determine to hide behind the screen and watch the next interview between the two young people for themselves.

We have already learnt a great deal about Kate's character before reaching this scene. Here we see her plainly in command of the situation, enjoying her power over Marlow and very cleverly playing her fish, already well and truly hooked. We also see again her sense of fun in her relish of the ridiculousness of the situation and her ability to act the part she has chosen for herself.

SUMMING-UP

These answers will have shown you how to go through a scene

from beginning to end, leaving out nothing but high-lighting the important points. English grammar is often not taught in schools nowadays but for those candidates who have some idea of the way a sentence is built up, it is useful to remember that less important points can be tucked away in subordinate clauses, whereas striking points need main, or principal, clauses. The first example of this comes early in the second *Julius Caesar* question, 'While they are being admitted' — not important — 'Brutus shows his dislike of concealment' — important, and so expressed in a main clause.

You will have found many little quotations worked into the narrative and enclosed in quotation marks, which give the 'echo' of the actual scene the examiners hope to find. It is just as necessary to provide this in prose as in poetry, though nobody is expected to learn long prose passages by heart. In the *She Stoops to Conquer* answer, a single word like 'mercenary' is used for this purpose and no quotation is more than five words long, most have only three or four. In this question we again see the comparatively unimportant happening reported in a subordinate clause while the point to be emphasized needs a main clause, for example 'After some whispering between the old fathers' — not essential — 'Marlow declares he is determined to stay' — a vital point.

With regard to the second part of these questions, this can be dealt with very briefly as, obviously, far the greater proportion of the marks will be awarded for the first part. A single short paragraph may be enough to contain it, as in the Goldsmith answer; it will never be necessary to write at length. Be careful, though, to notice exactly what you are asked for and not to waste precious time giving unnecessary information.

3 Character Study Questions

INTRODUCTION

This type of question is very common at both levels and it is inexplicable and disappointing that it is often so badly done. Many candidates evidently consider that they have been invited to 'tell the story' of characters, rather than analyse their characteristics. They painstakingly begin at the beginning of the novel or play and go through to the end, pointing out all that a character does, or all that they can remember, but completely failing to discuss motives; there is no suggestion of what qualities are driving on or restraining the character, making a person loved or hated, interesting or dull, admirable or contemptible and so forth. We form our opinion of a literary character from words and actions and, to a certain extent, from what other people say and feel. It is a good idea, when preparing a novel or play, to have a page headed with the name of each important character and to make notes as you read of actions or words which indicate, for example, selfishness, generosity, humour, honesty, hypocrisy or whatever it may be, adding, for your consideration later, any remarks you find made about the characters by the people who know them. As in real life, such comments may prove to be perceptive and well-founded or quite untrue and uttered with some ulterior motive in view; you will only be able to decide about these when the whole picture is finished. These notes will provide a very helpful basis for your character studies, indicating clearly, as they will, the less obvious facets of everybody's personalities as well as their dominant traits. When you come to arrange these notes into some sort of shape as a character study, you will present the characteristics in what seems to you their order of importance and most probably not the order in which you discover them as you read the book. If ambition strikes you as being a man's or a woman's outstanding characteristic, as may be the case with the Macbeths, then you will deal with that first, as fully as you can, citing ambitious deeds, quoting ambitious words and maybe reporting what other people in the play or novel have said on this subject. Your next paragraph will deal with what seems to you to be the character's second most striking characteristic and so on.

At the end, to strengthen and confirm all you have said, you will briefly sum up the man or woman concerned, making sure that you stress the really important points. It is, of course, much easier to do this with 'unbalanced' types such as Uriah Heep or Iago or Volpone, than with the less eccentric characters. Often a question on character is not a straightforward request for a character-study but something rather more complicated, calling for some skill in the presentation of your material. However, if you have the main points of each character firmly in mind, you should not have much difficulty in deciding the best way to manipulate these to comply with the question's requirements. This is simply a matter of arrangement. Basically, what the examiners want to find out, however the question may be worded, is that you know the men and women in the novels and plays you have studied, that they are alive and real to you, and that you can convey your understanding of their personalities and motivations in a vivid and convincing way, remembering always to support your own views by 'quotation from and close reference to the text'. More answers involving character studies, complete or partial, will be found in other sections of this book, where they seem more fittingly to belong.

QUESTIONS FOR FIRST EXAMINATIONS

PYGMALION

EXPLANATORY NOTE

Shaw based his play on the myth of Pygmalion of Cyprus, who carved a statue of a beautiful maiden and then fell in love with it. He persuaded the goddess Aphrodite to bring the sculpture to life and he then married her, having given her the name Galatea.

In Shaw's play, Professor Higgins, an expert on phonetics, who represents Pygmalion, takes into his home a Cockney flower-girl, Eliza Doolittle, who represents Galatea, and teaches her to talk 'like a Duchess', successfully passing her off among his Society friends as a lady of high birth. He has 'created' this beautiful, polished creature from the humble earthiness of the street flower-seller, as Pygmalion created his bride from the clay he modelled but, unlike Pygmalion, as soon as his experiment is brought to a conclusion, Higgins loses all interest in the girl.

QUESTION

'Professor Higgins's character is full of contradictions.' Say how

far you agree with this opinion of Higgins, supporting your answer
by reference to the events of the play.

ANSWER

If we read the stage directions only in *Pygmalion* we shall have an
almost complete picture of Higgins's character, without needing to
study the play at all, and these directions certainly make it plain
that there are contradictions to be found in him. He is 'overbearing but good-humoured', he indulges in 'genial bullying',
he acts 'violently' and rises 'in a fury' or 'with stormy petulance',
yet the striking of the church clock can remind him of the voice
of God rebuking him. His intolerance and impatience are stressed
in these directions but Shaw tells us he is 'likeable even in his
least reasonable moments'. It may be that his creator has more
affection for him than students of the play. An examination of
his words and actions will show how fundamental these apparent
contradictions in his character are and whether he really is as
complicated as the quotation in the question suggests.

Perhaps the most outstanding of his characteristics is his lack of
consideration for other people. Not only Eliza but his mother and
the Eynsford-Hills are treated by him with an extraordinary failure
of understanding and disregard of their feelings. He habitually
discusses Eliza in her presence as if she were an inanimate object.
'Take her away and clean her!' 'She'll only drink if you give her
money.' 'She's incapable of understanding anything.' The most
striking example of this is after his successful passing off of Eliza
as a Duchess when he cries 'Thank God it's over!' and is 'as-
tounded' at Eliza's rage. He is completely lacking in concern about
what is to become of her and talks unfeelingly of finding someone
to marry her off to — he shows the same insensitivity to the poor
Eynsford-Hills. 'You'll do as well as anybody else,' he tells them.
He sums up this very unendearing trait in his disposition himself,
'I can't change my nature and I don't intend to change my manners'.

It is possible to set against this his generosity. He throws a
handful of money into Eliza's basket and offers her his silk hand-
kerchief when she cries. 'Pay her whatever is necessary,' he orders
and he keeps her in the comfort of his own home during his
experiment with her. He offers Doolittle £10 for her instead of
the £5 he asks and it is made evident that he is not mean or
grudging with money. But he is a rich man and never gives anything that costs him something to part with. There is no thought-
fulness or personal concern in his generosity; he does not even

know exactly what or how much he is giving. Does this really provide a contradiction to his lack of consideration for others or is it, in fact, the same characteristic looked at from another point of view?

Higgins's immaturity is another of his very marked characteristics. How much his mother is to be blamed for this is a matter of opinion. She still treats him as a small boy, orders him about: 'Be quiet, Henry', and 'Sit down, dear, and listen to me', and praises him when he is obedient. He is a great eater of sweets and chocolates. His manners at his mother's house are shocking; he shows off like the spoilt child he is and behaves in schoolboy fashion, muttering imprecations and 'swooping' on his mother and dragging her to the ottoman. He seems never to have matured sexually. Shaw tells us he doesn't make much distinction between men and women. Eliza's proximity and affection leave him totally unmoved, his idea of a lovable woman is one as much like his mother as possible. 'I shall never get into the way of liking young women; some habits lie too deep to be changed', he says, and, obviously uncomfortable at this topic of conversation, he rises abruptly and walks about, 'jingling his money and his keys in his trouser pockets'. His mother is evidently saddened by her perception of her son's inadequacy in this respect and when he tells her that he is not having a love affair with Eliza, her reply is 'what a pity!'.

There is not much that can be seen as a contradiction of Higgins's emotional immaturity except his highly developed intellect and the shrewdness he shows in his negotiations with Doolittle, when he pretends to wash his hands of the whole matter of Eliza's education in order to persuade Doolittle to agree to his proposal.

His humour is very much that of the schoolboy and usually shows his habitual lack of concern for people's feelings — 'uproariously amused' and 'laughing uproariously' are phrases used of him. He is inconsiderate when he laughs at Mrs Eynsford-Hill's obvious pride at having been brought up at Largelady Park and positively rude and hurtful in his laughter at Eliza's suggestion that she should teach phonetics.

Only once are we told that he speaks 'gently' to Eliza. Generally he seems to be on a different wave length from her. We are told he is 'shocked and hurt', even 'deeply wounded', at Eliza's reaction to his treatment of her on the night after the garden party but to the audience Eliza's reaction is entirely comprehensible and it is Higgins whose behaviour seems odd and lacking in normal human feelings. His friendship with Pickering is really no more than a collaboration over work. In his arrogance he cries pathetically,

'I can do without anybody. I have my own soul; my own spark of divine fire', but we see him as pitiable, missing the best in life, and so obtuse that he does not even realise his loss. The picture Shaw gives us of Professor Higgins is, in fact, a well-drawn and consistent one and the apparent contradictions are all an integral part of a convincing whole.

GREAT EXPECTATIONS

EXPLANATORY NOTE

An orphan boy called Pip is brought up by his sister and her husband Joe, the village blacksmith. An eccentric lady, Miss Havisham, living near Pip, arranges that he shall come and play from time to time with the little girl, Estella, whom she has adopted. When Pip learns from Miss Havisham's lawyer, Mr Jaggers, that he has 'great expectations' and is to be removed from his humble home and educated as a gentleman, he believes Miss Havisham to be his benefactress and hopes one day to marry Estella. He never thinks of the escaped convict, Magwitch whom he once helped years before, but it is, in fact, Magwitch who, having made a fortune in Australia, has determined with the aid of Mr Jaggers, who is also his lawyer, to repay Pip for his kindness by making him rich and enabling him to take his place in a social class far higher than that he was born into.

Biddy, the young girl who helps to teach at the village school and who eventually marries Joe after the death of his first wife, always exerts an excellent influence over Pip. Mr Pumblechook is another of the villagers.

For candidates who have not yet read any Dickens this is a very good book to begin with. The plot is interesting and exciting, the characters easily grasped, and the abundant humour relieves a story which is often sad and even cruel.

QUESTION

What impression does Dickens create of the appearance and character of (a) Estella or Mr Jaggers and (b) Biddy or Mr Pumblechook? Describe the part that each of the characters you choose plays in the story.

ANSWER

(a) Estella
Our first picture of Estella is of a very pretty little girl and her beauty is emphasized all through the book. We see her 'delicately beautiful in her furred travelling dress' and at the end, although 'the freshness of her beauty" is gone, 'its indescribable majesty and indescribable charm' remain. We are given no more detailed

description than this, save for the mention of her fingers as she works which betray that she is Molly's child.

Her character appears to have no depth. As a child she is very proud, self-possessed, scornful, disdainful. She comments on Pip's coarse hands and thick boots and feeds him as if he were a dog, laughing 'contemptuously' at him and 'taunting' him. She is capable of unexpected and provocative behaviour, telling the bewildered Pip, 'You may kiss me if you like'.

At first the grown-up Estella seems changed to Pip but there is really no difference. She still lures him on, 'proud and wilful as of old'. We see her laughing, apparently with real enjoyment, but this is 'very singular' as there is nothing humorous in the situation. Her 'cold careless smile' always chills Pip and her 'self-possessed in-difference' strikes to his heart. She, herself, attributes her pride and hardness to Miss Havisham, whose puppet she has become, 'set to wreak her revenge on men'. She shows some sort of in-tegrity in refusing to deceive Pip, but she, who cannot love even the woman who has brought her up, is totally incapable of under-standing his consuming love for her. She shows him 'an unmoved countenance', declares she has no heart, regards his passion 'with incredulous wonder' and enters into an inexplicable marriage with Bentley Drummle, a boor without a redeeming feature. Very unconvincingly at the end of the book, Estella is shown saddened and softened, weeping, with her formerly insensible hand now friendly, a woman who has been bent and broken into a better shape. But for us she remains a cardboard figure, without life or credibility.

She provides the unsatisfactory love interest for Pip throughout the book and is the link between Miss Havisham, Jaggers and Magwitch but her comings and goings, once she leaves childhood behind, are never of much interest and it is impossible to under-stand how and why she so powerfully dominates Pip's life.

(b) Mr Pumblechook

Mr Pumblechook, a corn-chandler, and seed-merchant, is as unpleasant in appearance as in character. He is a 'large, hard-breathing, middle-aged, slow man, with a mouth like a fish, dull, staring eyes, and sandy hair, standing upright on his head, so that he looked as if he had just been all but choked, and had that moment come to'. Sometimes he indulges in 'a fat sort of laugh', perhaps when 'mellowed by gin'. There are various suggestions that he drinks too much.

He is interfering and insensitive, everlastingly telling Pip to 'be grateful, boy, to them which brought you up by hand' and making him do unnecessary mental arithmetic. His swollen-headed self-importance often makes him ridiculous, as when he freely hands round the wine he has just given as a Christmas present. His conceit is always apparent. His untruthfulness is staggering as when, for example, he pretends he knows Miss Havisham and her house, and lets everyone believe that Pip's apprenticeship is all his doing. He is referred to as 'that basest of swindlers' and 'fearful impostor'. When Pip's Great Expectations are revealed, he is all over him, 'My dear young friend', and claims to be responsible for his good fortune. He gives up his own room for Pip to dress in, provides clean towels, and is 'ecstatic' at Pip's so distinguishing him. At Mrs Gargery's funeral 'the servile Pumblechook' in very ostentatious mourning-garb nevertheless stuffs himself with the eatables provided. Our last glimpse of him is of a man 'with the air of a benefactor who was resolved to be true to the last'.

Mr Pumblechook plays no part in the development of the plot but he adds a great deal of humour to a story which is often sad and harsh. All he does is pose and posture. The tale of Pip and his Great Expectations would be exactly the same if he were absent from it, yet curiously enough he is more real and life-like than either Estella or Mr Jaggers, whose roles are far more significant and he is more likely than they are to remain indelibly impressed upon the memory of the reader.

ALTERNATIVE ANSWER

(a)   Mr Jaggers
We are given a detailed description of Mr Jaggers, a 'bulky man of an exceedingly dark complexion', 'with an exceedingly large head and a corresponding large hand'. He is prematurely bald on top and has bushy black eyebrows, overhanging deep-set, sharp, suspicious eyes. His chin is 'stubbly'. The smell of scented soap accompanies him wherever he goes.

He has various noticeable mannerisms — he uses his pocket-handkerchief to terrify his clients, beginning to blow his nose, then pausing while waiting for his victim to incriminate himself. He likes 'taking a bite at his fore-finger' and habitually stands with his back to the fire.

He treats his clients despotically and looks at Joe as if he recognizes him as the village idiot. We are told that 'Mr Jaggers never laughed', though his creaking boots sound as if they are laughing. However, he once 'smiled openly' when being told about Wemmick's home and the Aged Parent.

His office and perhaps the majority of his clients too reflect his personality, his 'determined reticence', his 'cold presence'. He is 'more in the secrets of every place', than anyone else but reveals nothing. His motivation is doubtful for his attempt to play God with Estella's life. Spider-like, he draws character after character into his web, but his reasons are more complicated than the spider's. Presumably they are love of power and enjoyment of intrigue. His home life, with Molly as house-keeper, seems as devoid of warmth and comfort as his office, his everlasting hand-washing is, one assumes, a manifestation of a feeling of guilt, the scented soap he uses, perhaps, a pathetic unconscious bid for the gracious living he so totally lacks.

Mr Jaggers plays a very important part in the plot. Because he is Magwitch's solicitor, and Miss Havisham's, and becomes Molly's employer and later Pip's guardian, he know everyone's secrets and links all the main characters together. As a good lawyer should, he keeps everyone's secrets but he gives the impression of enjoying the misunderstandings which thus arise. It is all he has to enjoy, the best things in life seem all to have passed him by.

(b) Biddy

We see Biddy, as we see Estella, emerge from childhood to woman-hood. Both are deprived children growing up without the warmth and security of normal family life but whereas Estella appears to be permanently warped by her unnatural upbringing, Biddy develops and matures into a deservedly happy wife and mother.

As a little girl she is 'most noticeable in respect of her extremi-ties', her hair, hands and shoes are always in need of attention, except on Sundays. She has a high, shrill, monotonous voice but, in spite of this, is able to interest and discipline her pupils in the village school. She inspires confidence; Pip says 'I told poor Biddy everything' and she is sympathetically quick at understanding what the paralysed Mrs Gargery is trying to communicate about Orlick.

Unlike Estella she changes very much as she grows up and becomes 'pleasant, wholesome, sweet-tempered'. She has always been obviously intelligent but reveals herself as capable of master-ing whatever comes her way from domestic chores to blacksmith's work. She is extremely sensible about Pip's pretensions to gen-tility, kind, comforting and selfless in her behaviour towards him, 'the wisest of girls'. We see her at her best when the snobbish Pip suggests that she should try to improve Joe's education and manners and she shows her own true and right priorities. Joe sees her as 'ever right and ready'. She genuinely grieves for Mrs Gargery and at her funeral we see her, now 'very neat and modest in her black dress', behaving in a quiet and helpful way. She has no illusions about Pip and his promised future visits to Joe; nobody sees straighter then Biddy. Her loving heart finally finds fulfilment as the wife of the splendidly deserving Joe and the mother of his children.

Her part in the book is to be a warm, genuine foil to Estella's dead coldness, a teacher and then a confidante for Pip at a difficult moment of his life and a comforter to Joe, whose first marriage has been so harsh and unrewarding.

JULIUS CAESAR

QUESTION

State what you learn from the play about two of the following, illustrating your answer by quotations:— (a) Portia, from her conversation with Brutus; (b) Cassius, from the opinions of him expressed by (i) Brutus and (ii) Caesar; (c) Antony from his conversation with Octavius in Rome.

ANSWER

(a) Portia
After the conspirators have left Brutus's orchard in the middle of the night, his wife comes out to look for him. The first thing we learn about her is her great anxiety for her husband, who has been behaving in such an unusual way. She says that she has previously asked him 'What the matter was' but that he had refused to answer and she had finally ceased to question him, 'Fearing to strengthen that impatience which seemed too much enkindled, and withal hoping it was but an effect of humour'. These words of hers show her womanly good sense and understanding.

Again she begs, 'Make me acquainted with your cause of grief', and refuses to accept his explanation that he is 'not well'. She knows that he has some worry within his mind and reminds him that, as his wife, she 'ought to know of' it. Evidently she takes her marriage very seriously. But she is a Roman wife and looks up to her husband as her lord and so she submissively goes down upon her knees on the damp grass to beg him to confide in her. Again she refers to her marriage vows and asks him if he thinks of a wife as somebody only to get his meals, sleep with him, and talk to him occasionally. 'If it be no more, Portia is Brutus's harlot, not his wife'. Brutus tells her that of course she is his wife in every sense of the word, and very dear to him.

Portia next says that, though she is only a woman, she is an exceptional one because she is the daughter of Cato and the wife of Brutus and so must be 'stronger than' other women. To prove this she shows him a wound she has inflicted on her own thigh, saying that if she can 'bear that with patience', she can certainly keep her husband's secrets. This episode shows us her courage and fortitude and her determination to convince her husband that he must share his secret with her, which, in fact, he promises to do.

So in this little scene, we see Portia's love for her husband, her respect for her marriage vows, her tact and understanding and her courage and resolution.

(b) Cassius
The first thing Brutus tells us about Cassius is that he numbers him among his 'good friends', and later in the same scene he addresses him as 'my noble friend'. At other times he goes so far as to call him 'good brother', so undoubtedly he feels great affection for him.

In the scene in Brutus's tent at Sardis, when he quarrels with Cassius, he forgets for a moment this friendship. Because he is angry with him he sees only his faults. He tells Cassius's slave, Pindarus 'Your master, Pindarus, In his own change or by ill officers, Hath given me some worthy cause to wish Things done, undone' and to Lucilius he talks of Cassius as a 'hollow' man.

When the two generals are alone, Brutus immediately taxes Cassius with having 'an itching palm', apparently quite an unjust accusation. The next fault Brutus accuses Cassius of, when Cassius is infuriated by the last charge, is having a bad temper, or, as he calls it, 'a rash choler', and he adds insultingly, 'Shall I be frightened when a madman stares?'

Next he charges Cassius with 'vaunting' (boasting) that he is a better soldier than Brutus, which Cassius has never said. He also calls him 'covetous', for keeping money back which he should have sent to Brutus. At the end of this sad scene, however, the two 'brothers' are reconciled and when Brutus and Cassius bid each other farewell, on Cassius's birthday, Brutus gives us a truer view of his feelings for his friend, when he calls him 'thou noble Roman' and later on that day, during the battle of Philippi, he stands over Cassius's dead body and says 'It is impossible that ever Rome should breed thy fellow'.

Caesar does not say very much about Cassius. He distrusts his 'lean and hungry look' and declares to Antony 'such men are dangerous'. Antony laughs at him but Caesar is not convinced. He says he is too great to be afraid of any one,

'Yet if my name were liable to fear
I do not know the man I should avoid
So soon as that spare Cassius.'
He goes on to add that Cassius is a great reader, and is capable of
seeing through men's deceits straight into their hearts. He does not
enjoy the theatre or music. 'Seldom he smiles' and when he does,
it is in a scornful way.

Caesar realises that this type of man can never rest while he
beholds 'a greater than himself' and it is for this reason — Cassius's
jealous ambition — that he considers Cassius dangerous.

(c)   Antony
We learn a great deal about Antony's character from his conversation with Octavius in Rome. First we learn his utter callousness
when, without a moment's hesitation, he marks his sister's son
down to die. 'Look, with a spot I damn him.'

Next we see his unscrupulousness with regard to the third of the
triumvirs, Lepidus. He has used Lepidus up to now as a necessary
part of his plans but the moment has come when Lepidus is in his
way and without any regret he is prepared to sacrifice his collea-
gue 'and turn him off'. He now calls Lepidus 'a slight, unmeritable
man' and when Octavius defends him, he says that he has more
experience than the youthful Caesar and knows that such men as
Lepidus are fit to be thought of 'But as a property'.

However, the last thing we learn about Antony in this scene is
his cleverness as a leader when he gets down to working out a plan
whereby 'covert matters may be best disclosed And open perils
surest answered'.

NB   All three parts of the question have been answered here,
although only two are asked for.

SUMMING-UP

In these answers you will have seen that the most prominent
characteristics have been examined first and at greater length than
other traits which show themselves only occasionally or perhaps
only once. Shaw does much of the student's work for him in his
stage-directions, stating plainly what good points and failings his
characters possess. Dickens and Shakespeare are not so considerate
and you will have to puzzle them out for yourselves. Again you
will see the short quotations worked into the answers, such as
'a fat sort of laugh', not hard to remember. However, without

some sort of preparation such as is suggested in the introduction to this section, you are unlikely to remember any prose quotations. If, as you read, you note down all the instances of qualities shown, such as Estella's scornfulness or Biddy's sympathetic nature, and each time add to your note the three or four words which encapsulate this quality, you are already half way to remembering these words and, when you come to revise, you can make sure of them. If this sounds like hard work, that is just what it is and you will not achieve a good grade without it.

4 Appreciation Questions

INTRODUCTION

It is necessary to know exactly what the word 'appreciation' means when used in Literature examination papers. Candidates very often mistakenly assume that they are being asked to write nothing but praise of the given poem and this may lead them to produce a string of gushing insincerities, which gives the examiner no indication of the real extent of their understanding of the poem's qualities.

'Appreciation', in the context of examination questions, means 'a critical estimate'. Candidates are being invited to consider the poem for themselves and say what they think about it. For first examinations, the set poem will always be taken from one of the prescribed selections or anthologies and candidates will therefore presumably have studied it with the help of a teacher during their preparation for the examination. It is common sense to suppose that if the examiners who chose the set books and then set the paper thought the poem good or important enough to include, it is unlikely to be an excessively poor specimen; it may be presumed to have good qualities. But that is not at all the same thing as saying that it is a poem of outstanding excellence which can only be praised from start to finish. Some poems in the anthology will seem more likely to live — if that is the test of the excellence of a literary work — than others. Some will have been chosen for one good quality, some for another. Different poems will appeal to different candidates. This is as it should be and gives scope for the expression of widely different opinions.

Each candidate must write honestly, if an answer is to have any value and what has already been said must be borne in mind, that there is likely to be something sufficiently interesting or unusual or technically skilled or emotionally stirring in the poem to warrant its inclusion in the selection. It ought to be possible to pin-point this quality and give it due praise, but there is no need to pretend to like everything. There may well be things in the poem which engender dislike or leave the candidate quite unimpressed.

At advanced level the poem will not usually be one which the candidate, except by happy chance, has seen before, nor can it be assumed that it has necessarily any merit at all. The candidate's own judgment must be relied upon.

The next matter to be considered is versification. Some teachers don't teach metre at all. Others bring their pupils up the school with a growing knowledge of the techniques of poetry writing. Candidates who are ignorant of metre and scansion can still consider the arrangement of the poem on the page and, in a general way, its rhythms and rhymes. The poem may be divided into verses of the same or different lengths, or it may not be split up at all. In any case, the poet had a reason for doing what has been done. A candidate must think out what this reason was and decide whether the poet has succeeded in fulfilling this intention. If the poem has not been split up, presumably in order to give it a continuous flow, consider whether it would have been easier to understand if it had been divided. If each verse encloses a separate thought, is this satisfactory, or possibly too jerky, contrived or rigid? If the thought runs from line to line or verse to verse, is this fluidity acceptable or possibly confusing? Questions like these can be answered by candidates who have no knowledge at all of metre. As far as rhythm is concerned these same candidates can decide whether the slowness, quickness, smoothness, jerkiness, or whatever it may be, of the rhythm is in accordance with the subject, whether it makes them feel like dancing or singing or lamenting or racing or crawling; the most important point to consider in this section is whether or not the rhythm helps the poet to get meaning and feeling across to the reader. The use or absence of rhyme can also be considered by candidates ignorant of metre. Rhyme produces an insistent beat, it is a form of linking lines, sometimes half-lines, and verses, it can be soothing or irritating. In a marching song, for instance, it is probably essential but in contemporary poetry it is seldom used. A candidate must think about the effect the rhyme has, whether it is helpful or otherwise to understanding and enjoyment of the poem. If no rhyme is used, this fact should be noted and the candidate should say why he supposes the poet preferred to do without it. Candidates who have been taught the principles of metre and understand the poet's manipulation of stressed and unstressed syllables for effect can use this knowledge in a brief comment. Simply to scan the lines or to say that they are iambic pentameters or anapaestic tetrameters is pointless; a candidate must show why he or she thinks the poet chose that particular metre. It must be explained that an inverted foot here or there lays stress on a certain word for a certain reason, or that occasional variations in the rigid metrical scheme produce a more natural or less monotonous effect, or, perhaps, in a poem about the sea, that the arrangement of stresses skilfully suggests the rise and fall of the waves. It is comments like these that the examiners hope to find.

QUESTIONS FOR FIRST EXAMINATIONS

'THE SOLITARY REAPER'

QUESTION

Write an appreciation of Wordsworth's 'The Solitary Reaper'.

ANSWER

This poem describes an incident which must have struck Wordsworth's imagination on one of his long country walks. He came upon a girl, reaping alone in a field and singing to herself as she did so. Her beautiful voice, reminiscent of the pure, natural notes of a bird, the lovely valley and the girl's rhythmic movements as she worked, all combined to stimulate the poet's imagination and lead his thoughts away to other scenes and singers.

He treats his theme with an appropriate simplicity and seriousness, investing the incident, by the use of such words as 'melancholy' and 'plaintive', with a feeling of sadness. He thinks the girl's song may have been of 'unhappy' things of 'natural sorrow, loss or pain'. He is tremendously moved by it, listening 'motionless and still' and retaining the song in his heart 'long after it was heard no more'.

The imagery used is entirely suitable to the subject. 'Overflowing' presents us with the cup-like shape of the valley, filled to the brim with the young girl's liquid notes.

In the second verse, the naturalness of her singing is emphasized by Wordsworth's comparisons of it first to the notes of the nightingale and secondly to those of the first cuckoo, arriving at the furthest outpost of these islands. In each case the emphasis is on the welcome accorded to the singers by their hearers, the nightingale is delighting 'weary bands of travellers in some shady haunt, among Arabian sands', and the cuckoo comes as the herald of summer. In each case, the birds are singing, like the Solitary Reaper, in lonely, quiet places where their notes can be enjoyed to the full and, again like the Reaper, they are completely unaware of their audience.

The third verse allows the poet to speculate on the subject of her song. Perhaps 'old, unhappy, far-off things and battles long ago' represent the ballads, passed on traditionally from mouth to mouth.

The diction throughout the poem is simple and has a natural dignity, befitting the theme. There are traces of the poetic diction Wordsworth rebelled against in 'lay' and 'whate'er' and 'o'er', even perhaps in 'yon'. 'Thrilling' is evocative of the power the Reaper's voice had to move the poet but there are very few words which, out of context, seem striking or unusual. It is Wordsworth's power of combining them in unforgettable phrases which produces the magic; 'the silence of the seas among the farthest Hebrides', 'old, unhappy, far-off things and battles long ago'.

The poem has four verses, each consisting of eight lines which are linked by a shifting rhyme scheme, ABCBDDEE in the first verse, ABABCCDD in the second and so on, this lack of rigidity according well with the girl's own untaught song. The easy iambic rhythm with its occasional variation — an inverted foot, like 'reaping' in the third line, or the feminine endings 'ending' and 'bending' in the last verse — also adds to the effect of simplicity and naturalness.

The poem makes, surely, much the same impression on the reader as the incident made on the poet. Words, imagery and versification are perfectly suited to the theme and leave the reader haunted by the beauty of the experience of which he has been made a part.

'THE DEAD'

QUESTION

Write an appreciation of Rupert Brooke's sonnet 'The Dead'.

ANSWER

Rupert Brooke's sonnet 'The Dead' is written in an idealistic tone. The octave deals with the young men known to Brooke who have given their lives in the war. He sketches the beauty and happiness of their youth; the pleasures they have known; the sensations they have experienced. After the abrupt 'All this is ended', the sestet seems for a moment to have departed altogether from the theme, until we realize that in Brooke's lovely description of scenes from Nature in summer and winter he is presenting these young men's lives to us once more in the form of imagery.

This is a romantic poem. The poet writes with love and admiration of his friends who have died for England and presents to us only their best side. We see them happy, good, surrounded by affection and enjoying the use of their senses to the full. 'These had seen movement, and heard music', 'touched flowers and furs and cheeks'.

We cannot imagine these young men dirty, dishevelled, angry, swearing, sadistic as other War Poets picture the soldiers. All is charming and admirable. In the imagery too, the descriptions capture us with their beauty. 'There are waters blown by changing winds to laughter and lit by the rich skies, all day'. There is nothing here to remind us of the conditions in the trenches of which we have learnt from many of Brooke's fellow-poets. We are left at the end of the poem with a feeling of stillness, purity and peace to comfort our grieving hearts.

This poem is so full of imagery that most of the striking words occur in metaphors. However, leaving these aside for the moment, Brooke's diction still merits examination. When he says his companions went 'proudly friended', the first word gives us a whole picture of the upright honourable young men, delighting in their closeness to others of the same sort, and 'friended', in spite of its unusualness, does not seem forced as if the poet had been compelled to use it to rhyme with 'ended'. Again, 'unbroken' is perhaps a strange epithet to apply to 'glory' but here it gives the effect of stillness and wholeness for which the poet is aiming. 'A gathered radiance' makes us think and concentrate our attention in an effort to understand exactly what the poet means by 'gathered', presumably he means a radiance gathered together into one complete whole; in fact, the 'unbroken glory' expressed in a different way. The last striking word in the poem is 'width', amongst 'glory' and 'radiance' and 'shining peace'. Here the poet is evidently trying to convey the vast extent of the white light into which the dead have passed.

Rupert Brooke uses a great deal of imagery in 'The Dead', some of it fairly ordinary and not particularly noticeable, as the hearts that were 'woven of human joys and cares', 'washed' by sorrow, and 'the waves that dance'. But we shall not easily forget the personification of frost, who 'with a gesture stays the waves'. 'Wandering loveliness' too is memorable and the word 'wandering' seems to bring the whole movement of the sea before our eyes.

The sonnet is an irregular Shakespearean one, rhyming ABAB/CDCD/EEFG/FG and the fourteen iambic pentameter lines enclose the poet's thought most satisfactorily.

'BAVARIAN GENTIANS'

Write an appreciation of D.H. Lawrence's 'Bavarian Gentians'.

ANSWER

This poem which describes feelingly the dark blue beauty of the flowers the poet has beside him as he sits at home one day in late September has sadder depths which are revealed by a more penetrating study. The blazing blueness of the petals reminds him of a torch, a torch, as it were, 'giving off darkness' rather than light and leading to the Underworld. In classical legend, Pluto, The King of the Underworld, carried off Persephone to be his bride and live in his gloomy kingdom. Her grief-stricken mother Ceres, Goddess of the earth's produce, sought her ceaselessly, neglecting her duties and so the growing plants sickened and died and for the first time the season of winter was known. Pluto eventually allowed Persephone to return to earth for half of each year, our Spring and Summer, but compelled her to go back to him for the period we know as Autumn and Winter and at her departure all plant life on earth begins to die. Lawrence embodies this legend in the heart of his poem, believing that he must shortly follow Persephone to the 'sightless realm where darkness is awake upon the dark', and he sees the gentians as illuminating his path and begs 'let me guide myself with the blue, forked torch of this flower, down the darker and darker stairs'.

The mood is melancholy but resigned. There is none of Dylan Thomas's passionately rebellious 'rage against the dying of the light'. Nor does Lawrence show fear, 'Lead me then, Lead me the way', he asks courageously.

The appeal to our eyes in this poem is little more than a vision of blazing blueness, 'Pluto's dark blue daze', and as, with Lawrence, we grope our way 'down the darker and darker stairs, where blue is darkened on blueness', we cease to be able to see even this 'and Persephone herself is but a voice, or a darkness invisible'.

The imagery is deliberately repetitive. Again and again we are presented with 'the blue forked torch of this flower', the 'torches of darkness', and each time the image comes, a 'torch-flower of the blue-smoking darkness' lights up our minds. 'Soft September' is a reminder of the world of light, Ceres' world, upon which Lawrence already seems to be turning his back to descend 'down the darker and darker stairs'.

The words Lawrence chooses are in themselves unremarkable, it is the way he combines them that gives magic to his phrases. 'Slow, sad Michaelmas' conjures up for us the death-bed of the year. 'Ribbed' gives us a picture of the faintly-lined petals; 'sight-less realm' and 'darkness invisible' present the bitter blackness of Hades and 'pierced with the passion of dense gloom' reveals that intense feeling which lives on in the seemingly dead land. Charac-teristically Lawrence makes some of his most telling effects by his sustained use of repetition; the ear is seduced to follow the in-tricate windings and unwindings of 'blueness' and 'torches' and 'darkness'.

The rhythm and length of line in this poem vary in accordance with the subject matter. The clear iambic statement of the first line is followed by a less regular line with one anapaestic foot and all through the poem the stress falls stumblingly, as it were, echoing the uncertain footsteps on the dark stairs; a regular punctual beat would be utterly out of place here and there is no rhyme, for the same reason. The poem is not a simple one to be grasped fully at a first reading, but it provides a most rewarding experience for those who are willing to lay themselves open to the images and feelings Lawrence is trying to convey.

QUESTIONS FOR ADVANCED EXAMINATIONS

MISCELLANY ONE AND MISCELLANY TWO

QUESTION

Choose the poem by Dylan Thomas you like best from the Selec-tions, write a critical appreciation of it and give your reasons for perferring it.

ANSWER

My favourite poem by Dylan Thomas from the Selections is 'Do not go gentle into that good night'. It is difficult to pick one and discard all the others one might have chosen, especially as so many of Thomas's poems deal, as this one does, with Death. However, the personal feeling in this poem, as Thomas watches his own father die, raises it above the others and the fact that it is so much less obscure than most of his work makes it far more pleasurable to read.

Thomas is presumably sitting by the bedside of his dying father as he writes and he is intensely moved by his father's passivity. Evidently the old man has been, when in full strength, as full of life and vigour as his son and now there is no more fight in him; he is submissively awaiting the end. Thomas implores him not to die like this but to fight every inch of the way, even though he knows he cannot win.

He gives examples to his father of various classifications of men, all of whom struggle for some reason or other against approaching Death. Wise men, while recognizing that their time has come, fight nevertheless because they realize 'Their words had forked no lightning'. Good men rage because they see how they might have done better in more favourable circumstances. Wild men who have lived life in their own heedless fashion 'do not go gentle' because they realize too late what wounds they have inflicted during their uncontrolled career. Men who have been solemn and serious resist Death in the hope of enjoying the gaiety they might have had. And in the last verse Thomas prays not for his father's final blessing, as most sons would have done, but for a blessing conveyed by curses and with 'fierce' tears, more in accordance with the old man's normal behaviour.

The diction in this poem is extraordinarily simple for Dylan Thomas. No words are used which are not readily understandable by any reader and a great many of them are monosyllabic. What is unusual about the diction is Thomas's use of one part of speech where we expect another. The 'gentle' of the title, which is often repeated in the poem, is an example of this, as we expect the adverb 'gently'. His use of paradoxical phrases too, such as 'blinding sight' and 'curse, bless' removes all possibility of prosaicness.

The imagery is striking and typical and improves from verse to verse. Old age itself is personified and, unexpectedly, urged to burn and rave. 'Forked no lightning' is a more successful metaphor for the wise men's failure to cause a sensation. The good men's 'frail deeds' which 'might have danced in a green bay' gives us a delightful visual impression of sunshine and glistening sea in contrast to the muted colours of the death chamber. The extravagance of the imagery of the wild men 'who caught and sang the sun in flight' is exactly right as an indication of the daring, ambitious, triumphant careers such men follow in life. And in the penultimate verse the 'grave men' who have neglected pleasure to follow more serious studies, suddenly have a blinding realization of the mistake they have made and know that their 'blind eyes' — eyes, perhaps, which have pored over manuscripts or figures and failed to see what they were missing — could have blazed 'like meteors' and enjoyed gaiety and brightness and a swift tempo of living totally outside their experience.

The form of the poem is, like the diction, extremely simple and accords very well with the subject matter. There are five three-line stanzas and a concluding four-line verse. The rhyme scheme is continued throughout the poem ABA ABA etc., and in the last verse there is an extra rhyming line ABAA which makes an effective conclusion. The metre is iambic on the whole with sufficiently numerous variations to break the monotony. The stresses on the first words of the third, fourth and fifth verses, for example, attract our attention to the different types of men the poet is considering. As has already been mentioned, a very large proportion of the words used are monosyllables which have the effect of slowing down the pace, in keeping with such a subject as the death of the old man. The frequent use of repetition is effective in two ways. It gives something of the effect of a prayer or invocation, suited to the occasion, and also rings in our ears almost as the tolling of the death bell.

Perhaps this poem is untypical of Thomas in its total lack of obscurity, of absorption in self, and of mention of any of Thomas's obsessions. It is unfortunate that his most popular poems are those most uncharacteristic of himself but so it seems to be. Certainly my chief reason for choosing this poem is that it has none of Thomas's most characteristic features but is a simple poem on a simple theme charged with normal human emotion and written in a simple rhythm which suits the subject perfectly.

'SUNK LYONESSE'

QUESTION

Write a careful study of the following poem, 'Sunk Lyonesse', paying regard to such matters as subject, form, style and total impression, and saying what you like or dislike about it.

In sea-cold Lyonesse,
When the Sabbath eve shafts down
On the roofs, walls, belfries
Of the founded town,
The Nereids pluck their lyres
Where the green translucency beats,
And with motionless eyes at gaze
Make ministrelsy in the streets.
And the ocean water stirs
In salt-worn casemate and porch.

Plies the blunt-snouted fish
With fire in his skull for torch.
And the ringing wires resound;
And the unearthly lovely weep,
In lament of the music they make
In the sullen courts of sleep;
Whose marble flowers bloom for aye;
And — lapped by the moon-guiled tide —
Mock their carver with heart of stone,
Caged in his stone ribbed side.

ANSWER

This poem gives the picture in words of King Arthur's City, Lyonesse, now sunk beneath the sea. There is no story, no human situation. The dying Sunday sunshine pierces down to highlight the tops of the tall buildings. The Sea-nymphs, staring through the clear greenness, bring sound to the quiet streets with the music of their lyres, while the water moves gently through windows and doorways. A fish finds his way by the light in his own head, while the nymphs continue their music and weep at its sadness in that sleeping city. The carved marble flowers will never fade, although their creator lies drowned and petrified by the continuous action of the salt waves.

The description is not broken up into verses, and the two long sentences balance each other. The uninsistent rhymes on the second, fourth, sixth etc. lines loosely weave the strands of the poem together. The rhythms are subtle and as unobtrusive as the rhymes, echoing the quiet rise and fall of the water, the push of the oncoming wave and the drag as it recedes.

The choice of words is all-important in a poem of this type, each being, as it were, a further brush stroke of the painter. This poet has selected his verbs with especial precision; 'shafts' is particularly effective with its association with a mine and its evocation of depths. 'Beats' for the movement of the light under the sea, by its appeal to the ear, gives us also the sound of the waves. 'Plies', emphasized by the inversion of the natural word order, gives a vivid impression of the fish's purposeful to-ing and fro-ing. Some adjectives are strikingly used. 'Foundered' of course gives us a comparison with a wrecked ship, 'moon-guiled' compactly sums up the moon's influence on the tides; 'sullen' is perhaps, the most arresting with its suggestion that there is no polite response to the Nereids' music. 'Sea-cold' carries a feeling of drowning and 'salt-worn', yet another compound, reminds us of the continuous, eroding action of the water. 'Unearthly' and 'lovely' fittingly describe the musicians. 'Casemate' is strikingly unusual and is probably chosen for the echoed vowel sound, as one wave echoes another, within the caves and vaulted chambers of this strange land.

The imagery in the poem is in accordance with the characteristic subtlety and unobtrusiveness seen everywhere – onomatopoeia is used to strengthen the impression given of the sea, 'stirs' and 'lapped', and, to make us hear the music, 'ringing wires resound' (the alliteration also contributes to the effect) and 'pluck their lyres'. The strangeness of the sea-nymphs, their difference from living girls, is conveyed by their 'motionless eyes at gaze', as if they were under a spell. The final picture of the drowned artist, turned to stone by the water's ceaseless restlessness is weird and unforgettable.

Colour is used very carefully, with the green of the water, the whiteness of the marble and stone and the sudden, bright fieriness of the one normal, living creature in that enchanted world, 'the blunt-snouted fish'.

The poet succeeds in his intention. We see the roofs and towers, gleaming whitely amidst the green, we hear the lapping of the water. (Predictably, perhaps, in a poem about Lyonesse, there are echoes of the *Morte d' Arthur*.) The deadness of the city comes over to us and the timelessness of its future. The poem is a miniature and aspires to be nothing greater; a small, delicate work of craftsmanship. As such I find it pleasing and memorable.

SUMMING-UP

Although these five poems differ so greatly, the method used in answering the questions is the same for all. First the theme is outlined – what the poem is all about – then comes an investigation of the poet's treatment of his theme, that is his choice of words and his use of imagery. The mood of the poem will be revealed by this examination, for instance the romantic nature of Rupert Brooke's sonnet or the sadness of 'Bavarian Gentians'. If you think there is any additional special point to make, such as Walter De La Mare's use of colour in 'Sunk Lyonesse', it may well come in here, before you go on to comment on the form and, if you can and think it appropriate, on the versification. Remember it is your own opinion of the poem that the examiners will find interesting and do not be afraid to say what you really think.

5 Compare and Contrast Questions

INTRODUCTION

This is another way of saying 'Point out the similarities and dissimilarities' between two poems or characters or scenes. It is a very straightforward type of question and one example should be sufficient to indicate the way in which it should be tackled.

First deal with the similarities — this is what 'compare' means — in what you take to be the right order of importance. There may be a great many, there may be only a few. It all depends on how much alike or how different the two poems or characters or scenes may be. Obviously there must be some striking likeness between the two, even if it is only superficial, for the passages to have been chosen at all for this type of question.

Next, list all the ways you can find in which the poems or characters or scenes differ from each other, that is what 'contrasting' them means. One may include subject-matter the other doesn't mention, one may make far more use of imagery or striking diction, one may arouse more feeling than the other, their tones may differ i.e. one may be humorous or cynical or factual or fantastic and the other something else. It would be impossible to enumerate all the differences that might be found. You will simply have to look at the two passages before you and see for yourself what strikes you. If it is two poems you are dealing with, the form may come in here, the way they are set out on the page, their metres and rhythms. (If they should both be sonnets, for instance, that, of course, would be a similarity.)

When you have finished all this, consider whether there are more similarities than differences, or the other way around. Possibly you will find an equal balance between the two. In any case you are going to need a short concluding paragraph or single sentence to state which situation you find and sum up clearly and simply the results of your detailed examination.

QUESTION

Compare and contrast 'Felix Randall' by Gerard Manley Hopkins with 'Evans' by R.S. Thomas.

ANSWER

These two poems have certain superficial resemblances.

Both poets are parish priests and are describing visits to sick parishioners. The poems are both about working-men and are called by these men's names. Felix Randall is a farrier, Evans a farmer. Illness has, in both cases, reduced their strong manly frames to shadows of their former selves. Gerard Manley Hopkins says of Felix Randall, 'Sickness broke him'. No longer is he 'powerful amidst peers', and by the question 'Evans?' with which he begins his poem, R.S. Thomas shows that he can hardly recognize the sick man, now 'stranded' on his bed.

Apart from these similarities, however, the poems are very different. In 'Felix Randall', Gerard Manley Hopkins is mainly concerned with the relationship which grew up between himself and the sick man. 'This seeing the sick endears them to us, us too it endears', and he mentions 'tears that touched my heart'. We are very conscious that Hopkins is a priest, vitally concerned with the soul of Felix Randall. He says of the dying man, 'Impatient, he cursed at first but mended, being anointed and all'. Even before his illness, Hopkins had numbered Randall among his flock and seen the beginnings of a new growth of spiritual life in him '. . . a heavenlier heart began some Months earlier, since I had our sweet reprieve and ransom Tendered to him'. And he prays for God's forgiveness for his dead parishioner's sins, 'Ah well, God rest him all road ever he offended'.

R.S. Thomas, on the other hand, reveals nothing of his priestly vocation in 'Evans'. He could have been any visitor 'many a time' descending the 'bare flight of stairs'. There is no mention of religion in the poem, no prayer for 'that sick man'. The poet first paints the 'stark farm on the hillside', in which the dying man lies, 'the gaunt kitchen With its wood fire, where crickets sang Accompaniment to the black kettle's whine'. Outside 'the thick tide of night . . . drifted about the walls' and 'the drip of rain' could be heard from 'the one tree'. But it is not the dreary bleakness of the farm's situation or the blackness of the night that 'appalled' the poet but 'the dark Silting the veins of that sick man'. After glancing round the farm and its surroundings, the poet's spot-light finally focuses on its real object and shines down squarely on the 'bleak bed' and the 'lonely' man lying there.

Both poets make some use of imagery and we find therein the differences we might expect between the learned, scholarly Jesuit and the simple Welsh country parson. There is nothing simple about Hopkins's sophisticated use of alliteration all through the poem, ending in the magnificent line 'Didst fettle for the great grey drayhorse his bright and battering sandal', which brings before our eyes the mighty steed with its heavy hooves and deafens our ears with the sound of its powerful stamp. His tortuous sentence-construction has to be puzzled out, as in 'How far from then forethought of, all they more boistrous years . . . .' and this, perhaps, further obscures the meaning of images which are not always immediately comprehensible. 'A touch which quenches tears' — is there, perhaps, the idea of a candle-snuffer here, whose light touch extinguishes the flame? We do not usually think of water (tears) as needing quenching but as being, itself, the quencher of fire. 'Our sweet reprieve and ransom', used for the bread and wine which secure these blessings for us, is much easier to follow. The repetition of 'pining' echoes the poet's pain as he watches the suffering man deteriorate.

R.S. Thomas, on the contrary, is almost child-like in his simplicity. 'The thick tide of night' gives us the idea of the darkness sweeping right up to the farm walls; 'rain like blood' perhaps needs more thought. The sick man would not have had a blood-drip fixed up in his cottage bedroom — these belong to hospitals — but somewhere Thomas has heard the dripping of blood, and, as he listens to the rain outside and watches the man's life draining away, the simile comes to his mind. It is an obvious progression from blood to the 'weather-tortured' tree but he leaves this source and turns back to the sea again for the imagery of his final lines. As sand silts up the streams and prevents the full flow of water, so the blood (once more) of the dying man flows sluggishly as the darkness of death impedes the circulation and, like the hulk of a ship hauled up the beach by some high tide and left there when the water recedes, the sick man lies 'stranded upon the vast And lonely shore of his bleak bed'.

The two poets are as different in their diction as in their imagery. Hopkins's compound and alliterative words, 'big-boned' and 'hardly-handsome' strike us in the first verse as being economically descriptive. The need to be alliterative seems sometimes to have influenced his choice of word: 'fleshed' for instance, but it deserves its place, expressing concisely the battleground where poor Felix's four fatal illnesses fought against him. 'Fettle' is an unusual but powerful substitute for 'prepare'. Only a scholar's confidence could deliberately choose 'heavenlier'. We have to consider why the forge was 'random', perhaps it means constructed haphazardly.

But R.S. Thomas's diction never puzzles us. There is not a word in his poem that Evans himself, could not have understood. His epithets emphasize the lack of softening touches at the farm, 'bare', 'gaunt', 'cold', 'bleak'. There is not much comfort around the dying man, in spite of the wood fire and the cricket's song. The onomatopoeic 'whine' appeals to our ears and 'smother' makes us feel the almost tangible bleakness. 'Appalled' is a strong verb and stands out here shockingly, linking with 'blood' and 'tortured' to suggest the agony suffered by the farm's lonely occupant. But the words are not individually remarkable; it is their combination in such phrases as 'stranded upon the vast and lonely shore of his bleak bed' which remains in our memories.

The versification of the two poets is in accordance with their general approach to their themes. Hopkins's poem is one of his own kind of sonnet; that is to say the poem is fourteen lines long but the lines are not iambic pentameters and the rhyme scheme, though a regular ABBA ABBA in the octave, has an irregular sestet, CCDCCD. He writes in hexameters and scatters the stresses as he pleases, often bunching them together in groups, as in the last two lines of the poem. He often runs on the sense from one line to the next '. . . began some Months earlier . . .' and evidently feels free to make what he pleases of the conventionally rigid form.

R.S. Thomas has two short verses, sixteen short lines in all, trimeters generally with some tetrameters among them. The rhythm is basically iambic but Thomas, like Hopkins, feels free to shift the stress in such lines as 'Of his stark farm on the hill ridge' and 'Weather-tortured. It was the dark'. Neither poet is in any way constrained by his metre; not one of Thomas's lines is end-stopped, so that the general effect of 'Evans' is conversational and reminiscent, whereas, in spite of his flouting of conventional metrical rules, Hopkins's poem seems carefully elaborated and worked over.

So, to sum up, in spite of the superficial resemblances there are many underlying differences between the two poems, perhaps the most striking being the lack of any reference to religion, or the spiritual state of his parishioner in R.S. Thomas's 'Evans'.

SUMMING-UP

You will have seen in the given answer that there are far more differences between the two poems than similarities. The first short paragraph has been enough to deal with the likenesses, the rest of the answer analyses the differences (including subject-matter, tone, imagery, diction and versification) many of which arise from the fact that one poet is highly educated and scholarly and the other a simple countryman. The last sentence pinpoints the most notable difference, considering that both poems are written by priests, the absence of any religious content in one of them.

QUESTIONS FOR FIRST EXAMINATIONS

'FELIX RANDALL' AND 'EVANS'

6 Questions Demanding the Expression of a Personal Opinion

INTRODUCTION

Questions of this type are more likely to occur at Advanced level and often present candidates with a serious problem. They feel that they 'ought' to think a certain way, that the examiners expect them, for instance, to like and admire a particular character, or a writer's powers of description or characterization, when, in fact, they do not. What are they to do? Are they to pretend, in order to please the examiners and so get high marks, or are they to write the truth as they see it, and perhaps fail?

In truth, this problem is only in their minds and has no existence in fact. The examiners are not concerned at all with what opinions the candidate may hold of a book, a poem, a character; what they are interested in is ability to express views, and support them by reference to or quotation from the text. It is for the presentation of a case, whatever that may be, that marks will be given.

Many candidates have a guilty belief and even state in their scripts, that, though a certain poem makes no appeal to them or some character is for them lifeless and unconvincing, this must be their fault, a defect in their critical ability. This is not so, at all. Personal taste varies; it is not 'right' or 'wrong' to admire or to dislike the Romantic Poets; some people do one, some the other. What matters is for candidates to know why they like or dislike this poetry and to be able to say so clearly, with plenty of illustrations from the text.

The specimen answers which follow on the advanced texts, *Miscellany One* and *Miscellany Two* (Selections from the work of Dylan Thomas), and C.P. Snow's *The New Men*, have been deliberately chosen to show views which candidates might feel were not the 'expected' ones; they would lose no marks on that account. Obviously candidates who are able to write with sincere and unqualified approval of the set writers should do so. The important thing in this type of question is to be honest and to be able to produce enough evidence from the text to make one's theory tenable.

'MICHAEL'

QUESTION

Give your impressions of the way in which Wordsworth's Michael met the 'heavy news' of Luke's disgrace and show how far his behaviour at this point in the story fits in with what we have learnt about him earlier in the poem.

ANSWER

Because Michael was sustained by the strength of his love for his son, he did not break down either mentally or physically when he heard the 'heavy news'. He continued with his daily work, as he always had done, and 'performed all kinds of labour for his sheep, and for the land'. Every now and then he went to 'that hollow dell' to work at building the sheepfold but it was believed by all his neighbours,
'That many and many a day he thither went
And never lifted up a single stone'.
They sometimes saw him 'sitting alone' there or accompanied by his faithful old sheepdog, 'lying at his feet'. For seven years he struggled on but 'left the work unfinished when he died'.

So we are left with the impression of an old man with such strength of character that he refuses to give way to his grief and break down but who cannot quite force himself to finish the work alone which he had planned to do with his beloved son.

This is really just what we should expect of Michael as we have come to know him. All through the poem his strength has been emphasized. We are told he was 'an old man stout of heart and strong of limb', and again that 'his bodily frame had been from youth to age of an unusual strength'. This is illustrated by what we know of his life. He was always out of doors, working on the land or tending his flock and those storms, which sent the traveller to seek shelter, sent Michael up to the hills to guard his sheep. His self-discipline, which forced him to keep going after the heart-breaking news of Luke's disgrace is revealed to us earlier in the poem when, after a hard day's work out of doors, instead of taking the evening off for rest or recreation, he immediately gets down to some other form of work,
'perhaps to card
Wool for the Housewife's spindle, or repair

Some injury done to sickle, flail or scythe'.

His diet too, is free from all self-indulgence, 'a mess of pottage and skimmed milk', 'oaten cakes' and 'plain home-made cheese'.

Michael's love for his son is made evident all through the poem. For the first two days of his life, while the baby slept, the proud father hung over him, blessing him. Then he took over the care of him as if he had been the mother, doing him 'female service' and we are told that if Michael's work had not taken him out of doors, Luke would have been brought up 'upon his father's knees'. The toddling Luke watched beside his father at the sheep-shearing, the five-year-old had his own little staff to control the sheep with, the ten-year-old boy accompanied his father up to the mountain tops, and they 'were as companions'.

This closeness reaches its height at their farewell meeting at the sheepfold, which was to be 'a covenant' between them and where the father told his son,

'whatever fate

Befall thee, I shall love thee to the last

And bear thy memory with me to the grave'.

This vow Michael most certainly kept.

So, from all we are told about Michael in the early part of the poem, we should expect his behaviour at hearing the 'heavy news' of his son's disgrace, to be exactly as Wordsworth describes it.

THE POEMS OF WILFRED OWEN

QUESTION

Which qualities in Wilfred Owen's poems in this anthology have you found admirable?

ANSWER

Wilfred Owen's wonderful descriptive power is, perhaps, what strikes us first and this is revealed in most of his poetry. Very often it is not only to our eyes and ears that he appeals but, like Keats, to our other senses too, to conjure up before us the pictures and the atmosphere he wants us to see and feel. In 'Exposure' Owen makes us aware of the deadly cold and the cruel winds, 'Our brains ache, in the merciless iced east winds that knive us . . . .' Our ears shudder at the 'rumbles' of the guns.

In 'Spring Offensive' we are given a temporary relief. It is May, the soldiers 'watched the long grass swirled, by the May breeze, murmurous with wasp and midge' and 'the buttercup had blessed with gold' their heavy boots.

But it is, perhaps, in 'Dulce et decorum est' that we see Owen's descriptive power at its best. There is hardly a line which does not give us some ghastly picture, fill our ears with some heartbreaking sound. 'Bent double, like old beggars under sacks, knock-kneed, coughing like hags, we cursed through sludge', and very soon we hear 'the blood come gargling from the froth corrupted lungs', as the gassed man dies his horrible death.

Another characteristic of Owen's descriptive power frequently seen in his poetry is very clear to us in this poem. It is the dream-like atmosphere which makes so many of his poems memorable. In this poem, 'Dim through the misty panes and thick green light, As under a green sea I saw him drowning', and in 'Strange Meeting' we escape 'down some profound dull tunnel' where 'encumbered sleepers groaned, Too fast in thought or death to be bestirred'.

Leaving his power to describe and to create atmosphere, we may next examine his use of contrast, which is often extra-ordinarily effective. After the shocking realism of the soldier's end in 'Dulce et decorum est', with words such as 'obscene as cancer', 'vile, incurable sores', Owen suddenly reverts to the old, idealistic language of the young poets who went straight from school to war in its early days believing they were saving England and freeing the world from war for evermore.

'My friend, you would not tell with such high zest
To children ardent for some desperate glory
The old Lie: Dulce et decorum est
Pro patria mori'.

In 'Exposure' we see the contrast between the bitter hardships and dangers of the front, and the men's warm, peaceful memories of home in the sixth verse. In 'Strange Meeting' the man whom Owen had 'jabbed and killed' the previous day tells him in their eerie, dream-like tunnel of the loveliness so different from all they have experienced in war. 'I went hunting wild After the wildest beauty in the world.'

Sometimes Owen uses shock tactics to impress upon us what he wants us to grasp. In 'Insensibility' he startles us by taking the unconventional point of view that unfeeling, unimaginative, unpitying men are the lucky ones at the front:— 'Happy are men who yet before they are killed Can let their veins run cold . . . Happy are these who lose imagination'.

The end of 'Strange Meeting' is, of course, a shock to us when we first learn who the man confronting Owen is and such a line as the last one of 'Inspection' is bound to shock us too into a deep consideration of what Owen's message to us here really is.

Owen's style changes a good deal as he matures as a poet. To consider first his diction, this becomes steadily more realistic, more bitter, more brutal as the war goes on. He can show gentleness, and tenderness, as in 'Futility', where he talks of 'the kind old sun' and 'how it wakes the seeds' but his choice of words in 'Inspection' is colloquial, effective but totally lacking in beauty. '"Old yer mouth", the sergeant snapped and "Well, blood is dirt", I said'.

He occasionally uses an unusual word like 'fleers' and he makes exceptional use of monosyllables to slow down his verse as in 'To face the stark, blank sky beyond the ridge' and he often employs doublets like 'clutched and clung'. When necessary, he makes good use of onomatopoeia, as in 'Dulce et decorum est' 'guttering', 'choking', 'gargling'. His imagery is always interesting. In 'Exposure' he writes 'we hear the mad gusts tugging on the wires Like twitching agonies of men' and although he is appealing to our ears with the sound of the wind's ferocity, he also shows our eyes a terrible picture of men dying on the wire 'among its brambles'.

In 'Insensibility' 'they are troops who fade not flowers' and 'Chance's strange arithmetic Comes simpler than the reckoning of their shilling'. The first image is simple and we see the young, once vigorous boys mown down as garden flowers, in all their beauty, may be. The second more complicated image expresses tellingly that it is all 'the luck of the draw' who lives and who dies.

The last characteristic of Wilfred Owen's poetry which we have enjoyed is the impression of the personality of the poet, himself, which we have gained from reading his poetry. He shows his extreme sensitivity in his deep feeling for his men, his growing hatred of the cruel and futile war and in the fact that he so constantly and successfully appeals to our own senses.

His courage is everywhere apparent and his ironic humour makes a poem like 'Inspection' seem slightly less brutal than it might. The last personal characteristic of Owen's, implicit if not explicit in most of his poetry, is his sense of duty and responsibility, which sent him back to the front and to his death, although he had long ceased to believe in the rightness of the war.

These, then, are the qualities of Wilfred Owen's poetry which seem most admirable and which make us read and re-read his work with thoughtful attention.

THE NEW MEN

EXPLANATORY NOTE

This novel is concerned with the discovery of nuclear fusion and its immediate consequences. Much of the action takes place at Barford, where the
experimental work is actually being carried out. One of the scientists there,
Sawbridge, is, in fact, a spy, who is unmasked during the course of the novel.
Before the Barford team completes its work the news comes of the dropping
of the first atomic bomb on Hiroshima.

QUESTION

How successful do you consider C.P. Snow to be in the presentation of his minor characters?

ANSWER

Some great novelists excel in their plots, some have markedly
individual styles, some create unforgettable characters. Even if a
novelist is not pre-eminent for his characterization his principal
characters will almost certainly make some impact on his readers
but those whose creative imagination is outstanding in this particular aspect of novel-writing are equally remembered for all the
much less important people who are introduced into the story. Of
all English novelists Dickens is probably the greatest in this respect
and often his minor characters, in *Bleak House* for instance, are
actually more convincing and unforgettable than the major ones.
  C.P. Snow can certainly not be mentioned in the same breath as
Dickens as a creator of character. We are not here required to
examine the chief actors in his plot; these are Lewis and Martin
Eliot, Martin's wife Irene, and Walter Luke, but those lesser figures
who provide the supporting cast; the other scientists at Barford
and their wives, Sir Thomas Bevill and Sir Hector Rose, Sawbridge
the spy and Captain Smith, who comes to Barford to investigate
the leaking of information to a foreign power.
  Before deciding whether or not C.P. Snow is successful in his
portraits of these people, it is necessary to look at his methods of
portrayal. He does not vary his approach very much but follows
much the same pattern in every case.
  Very soon after the mention of a new character he always gives
us a description of that person's appearance. Evidently he believes
in the necessity of our being able to visualize everyone clearly.
There is no doubt that the feature which he personally finds most
striking is the eyes. Without exception he gives us a detailed
picture of everybody's eyes; readers who, perhaps are as much

impressed by other features may feel that he does not tell us enough about the rest of the characters' appearances to make them really rise up vividly before us.

Perhaps Sir Thomas Bevill is the most successfully portrayed of the minor characters. He is 'thin-shouldered, wispy, like an elderly clerk'. This really does present an image to our minds and his complete lack of self-importance is stressed; he kneels on the hearth-rug to build up the fire himself, with coal which he has fetched. Later we see him travelling in a crowded train instead of in a government car, and Snow again emphasizes his already expressed likeness to a clerk.

He is 70 years old, 'Polonius-like', and this aspect of him is elaborated when we learn that he has a 'talent for using two words where one would do'. He has a very individual laugh, a 'curious, internal, happy laugh, as though he were smothering a dirty joke'. His 'frank, ingenuous, blue eyes' are much more easily imagined and fit in much more acceptably with his character than some of the other extraordinary eyes described. This ingenuousness is seen in his enjoyment at being in the secret of the uranium project and his delight in the code-name for it, 'Mr Toad', at the mention of which he gives a smile which is 'frank, shy and eager'. There are many illustrations of his child-like quality, such as his offering a bag of 'Bikkies' round the railway-carriage.

Dining with the Minister at Pratt's, Lewis reflects that people call him 'unassuming, unsnobbish (he is the cousin of Lord Boscastle), realistic, gentle'. He agrees with the first three epithets but knows the last to be false; he is, in spite of the 'bit of an old woman' impression he gives, exceedingly tough. We see his strength of character, Lewis calls him 'gallant', when, in danger of losing his job and against his own interests, he uses his influence to convince Sir Hector Rose that Luke's team at Barford must be supported and, when his dismissal comes, he takes it bravely, refuses a peerage and still hopes to return to an influential post.

It all fits in; we are getting a picture of a recognizable human-being, the sort of man we have all met, and there is no jarring, discordant note in the description which we cannot reconcile with the rest.

Sir Hector Rose, the Permanent Secretary, does not come off so successfully. He is 'a man in the early forties, stocky, powerful and youthful-looking, his official black coat and striped trousers cut to conceal his heavy muscles', a man evidently with the means to employ a good tailor. 'The flesh of his cheeks shone as though untouched, and his face, hair and eyes had the same lightness'. This description of his face does not really show us what he looked like. Does 'untouched' mean 'unshaven' (because he had no need to shave)? His face, hair and eyes are light, we are told, not as illuminating an adjective as it should be here. What is a 'light' face? Later we get another description of him which helps us to understand, at least, 'untouched' in reference to his face, which is 'still unnaturally youthful, expressionless'. His eyes are still 'light'.

He is a typical bureaucrat, 'trained to politeness', and this is stressed many times. Although he has 'no taste for show', he does not approach anywhere near to Bevill's simple homeliness. He wields a great deal of power and behaves in a suitably ceremonious way, though he never stands on his own dignity. Even in war-time the flowers on his desk are renewed each day and he is careful to keep cigarettes to offer to his visitors, though he does not smoke himself.

He is a cool man and a just one, capable of eliminating personal considerations from a discussion, and of speaking with a 'sarcastic flick of his tongue'. Lewis dislikes and trusts him. Even when he first hears the tremendous news that the Americans already have a bomb, he speaks 'in a flat tone'. He is called a man of judgment because he is always 'one jump ahead of official opinion'. We once see him, after Puchwein's visit, 'troubled by self doubt' and, in spite of the insistence on his general 'lightness', on that occasion he gives Lewis 'a heavy glance' and almost commits himself to speaking 'off guard'.

All this adds up to no more than the presentation of a typical top civil servant, which would not be out of place in one of the seventeenth-century collections of 'Characters'. Rose is a cardboard figure with no life in him, whom we see only on duty. We cannot imagine his home and family or Rose himself in the capacity of husband or father — in short, he is totally uninteresting and forgettable.

Eric Sawbridge, by the very fact that he leaks scientific secrets of potentially enormous importance to a foreign power, is bound to attract our curious attention. Lewis happens to be present when he is interviewed at Barford for a job there and discovers that the young man comes from his own home town and attended the same grammar school. Even his name, to Lewis, had 'a flat, comfortable Midland note'.

He is twenty-four, 'large, heavy, mature, with a single thick line across his forehead, a very light blond, who might have been a Scandinavian'. When he is lying ill in hospital, his skin has, as when he is well, 'its thick Nordic pallor' but 'the bald patches of scalp shone through' and, at last comes the so far missing description of his eyes, 'his eyes were filmed over, half opaque'. Later he grows a moustache 'fair against the large-pored skin'. He is clever and not much interested in anything outside his work, a devoted scientist. He is profoundly affected by the failure of the first test at Barford, 'his mouth open with pain, like a Marathon runner's . . . he was nearly crying'. Politically he had belonged to a pro-Communist group at Oxford and had attended anti-war meetings in 1940 and 1941. His physical courage is in no doubt; in the hot lab, when one of the containers cracks and Luke and Sawbridge are poisoned, the former far more seriously so, Sawbridge 'carried Luke away from the rods' and rings the bell for help. In hospital he is a bad patient and greets Martin and Lewis when they visit him 'in a scornful and unwelcoming tone' and aggressively announces that he is quite all right and does not need visitors.

Lewis realizes that 'under the familiar loutishness' lies 'a bitter pride'; he could not have borne pity. Full of courage himself, he does not resent those who are not but he cannot bear it that Lewis and Martin are striding about in full health while he is confined to bed. Martin tries to talk to him about their common interest in Botany but, at this, Sawbridge breaks into a strange, long, controlled outburst of swearing which strikes Lewis as 'the voice of a man cursing his fate, dislikeable, but quite undefeated'. When this is over, as if he has released some tension in himself, he feels able to join in discussion with the others, about when the work at Barford will start again. As soon as he is allowed he returns to his job.

By this time his politics have apparently become considerably less militant and he speaks 'like a milk and water member of the Labour Party'. Lewis and Martin do not know whether he is still under investigation as a suspected spy or not until Captain Smith reveals that he knows he is the culprit, though the Russians would not have gained very much from his disclosures.

C.P. Snow's weakness at characterization prevents him from making enough of this exceptionally tense situation, when Lewis and Martin, knowing Sawbridge's guilt, have to arrange for him to be watched and Sawbridge who 'knew his danger' and shows it by his 'sullen pale face', his walking 'lightly and jaggedly' on tiptoe instead of with his usual 'heavy, confident clatter', works on as usual, looking through his 'opaque sky-blue eyes' with courage and contempt at those who are waiting to pounce on him.

Even during his interrogation by Captain Smith, Sawbridge is able to grin at Martin's schoolboy humour, nothing can daunt him, probably because his conscience is clear and he has no gnawing sense of guilt. He is a devoted and tremendously hard-working scientist, who had wept at the failure of the first test and had been satisfied with his share of the ultimate success. 'Science had its own imperatives, if you were working on a problem, you could not but crave for it to "come out".' Although his motive is not clearly understood, there is no suggestion that he has handed secret material over to the Russians for financial gain; he apparently believes he is doing his duty, 'it was by doing his duty to the Soviet Union that he would in the long run be doing his duty to the people around him'.

Martin recognizes his utter aloneness at this time, 'the loneliness of a man who was cutting himself off from his kind', and he plays on it to crack and then break Sawbridge and extract a confession from him. But there is no excitement, no tension, in the interrogation scenes. C.P. Snow gives us such sentences as 'Martin increased the strain', but we feel no sense of this, we are not sitting on the edge of our chairs as we read, but asking ourselves 'How much longer is this going to be spun out?'.

Our last sight of Sawbridge is in prison where he seems exactly as usual. Lewis sums him up 'Faith, hope and hate: that was the troika which rushed him on . . . .' He was a man of almost flawless courage, moral and physical. Not many men would have bent as little. This all suggests a compelling and appealing character, with whom we might feel great sympathy. As it is, we don't care one way or the other about him, nor have we ever been stirred by his own defection or his relentless tracking-down. It is almost unbelievable that Snow can make of a man potentially so intriguing, someone so dull. He utterly fails to get across to the reader what makes Sawbridge 'tick' and that is the interesting thing about anybody.

It would be impossible to go through all Snow's minor characters, examining them in this way. These three must serve as examples of the rest. They provide us with, in Bevill, a recognisable, though not very fully developed, Cabinet Minister, in Rose, a tailor's dummy or cardboard figure, and in Sawbridge, who might have been an absorbing psychological study, a Midlander who is presented as being as flat and dull as his own accent. We must, then, come to the conclusion, that Snow is not a very successful creator of minor characters.

QUESTION

What do you consider to be the most outstanding characteristics of C.P. Snow's style as seen in *The New Men*?

ANSWER

The style of novelists may, perhaps, be divided into two categories. There is the clear, lucid style which attracts no attention to itself, but allows the reader to see through it, as if it were clear water, to the plot and characterization, which the author is anxious to develop. The other kind of style never allows us to forget the personality of the writer, himself. He is obtrusively present in every scene he describes and, if he is not congenial to us, we may heartily wish for his occasional absence. If a book is written in the first person, as *The New Men* is, it may, of course, be argued that it is Lewis Eliot's style of which we are so conscious and not C.P. Snow's, but for purposes of this answer we shall have to hold C.P. Snow responsible for what Lewis records.

Snow chooses, on the whole, to use sentences of medium length, at his best, or very short ones at his worst. This denies any smoothness to his writing and much of it is unpleasantly jarring and jerky, as, for example, his description of Pratt's. Owing to the fact that there is not a single long sentence in the whole book, it is a waste of time to examine his sentence construction. His method is one brick at a time and he rarely piles up more than two or three. He has little use for descriptive clauses or phrases and seems to enjoy a clinical bareness.

His vocabulary is that of a learned man. That is to say he continuously uses words which would not be understood by people who left school at the earliest possible age, and had not done any serious reading since. He often chooses words of Greek or Latin origin and of this we need make no complaint. But when he is trying to write realistic dialogue, the sort of speech which friends or close relations use to each other, he seems to have no ear at all. We are amazed at such an exclamation as Luke's 'Glug glug' and at words like 'Jaw-bacons' and 'joggled' and the statement 'That's tipped you the wink', even allowing for the period in which the book is set. He has a particular fondness for technical terms. Naturally a man who is describing an important piece of scientific research will have to use such words as 'slugs of uranium'. But surely it is not necessary when dealing with Luke's illness, to tell us about his diarrhoea and vomiting or to use the expression 'a blow to the viscera'. Very often his words seem ill-chosen and unsuitable, as in the description of Irene, 'wailing for past love affairs', in a manner 'fervid, almost jaunty'. Often he seems to take pleasure in ugly, not particularly expressive words, such as 'high-pitched yelps of glee'. We can search in vain for beautiful or memorable language.

His images, for the most part, are in accordance with his vocabulary, commonplace, uninspiring and sometimes not even apt. 'It was like a greenhouse in the club kitchen' is far from illuminating and what exactly he means by saying 'the air quivered like a watermark' is by no means obvious. His comparison of the Eliot brothers' frustration with Scott's when he found Amundsen had raced him to the South Pole is one of his better images and the best of all is his description of the sun's making blazing shields of the windows. A sense of humour is as completely lacking in his imagery as it is in all other aspects of the book.

Every writer with an obtrusive style has his own idiosyncrasies and to the observant reader will leave his mark on every page. Perhaps the most striking of Snow's is his capacity for deadly dullness; it would have seemed impossible to make what is, after all, a spy story so totally unexciting and flat. This effect is partly achieved by his failure to make any use of colour except for the all-prevailing greyness sometimes expressed by the word 'leaden', with the whiteness of snow and an occasional touch of black as almost the only variations. Much of the action seems to take place during very foggy periods and though there are sunny days in the book and 'beautiful sunsets', they hardly succeed in piercing the gloom. One rather unpleasant use of colour is his constant reference to his women characters flushing to the bottoms of their necks. He does once mention 'red brick houses' and 'yellowish plutonium' and once we are almost stunned to find green and silver mentioned on the same page.

One exception to the general colourlessness is seen in his extraordinary preoccupation with eyes, especially blue eyes. He never fails to describe this feature of each of his characters, often more than once, but never in the least realistically. What are we to make of Irene's 'narrow treacle-brown eyes glinting under the heavy upper lids' or Martin's, 'dark blue hard, transparently bright', or Puchwein's which 'slanted downwards so that he always seemed about to weep'? Not one of these descriptions helps us to see the characters but rather they stand in our way.

Another characteristic of Snow's style is his habit of following a noun or pronoun by a string of adjectives, for example, 'I had known them rancorous before, morally indignant, bitter'.

However, possibly the most irritating of all his idiosyncrasies is his unnecessary insistence on explaining what a speaker means by the perfectly intelligible sentence he has just uttered. He does this over and over again and it must surely be considered as a serious defect since it suggests either that he has not expressed himself clearly through the mouth of his character, or that he is spinning out his novel by saying the same thing twice.

These, then, seem to be the outstanding characteristics of Snow's style and they do not add up to anything very enjoyable.

It is not that the other type of style, which attracts no attention to itself, is necessarily preferable — individualistic stylists such as Dickens, Hermann Melville and Charles Morgan do not grate on their readers and the personalities they reflect seem sympathetic. Snow's style just seems to rub us up the wrong way and manages to distract us from following the story he is so baldly telling.

7 Discuss and Illustrate Questions

INTRODUCTION

Questions often begin with the words 'Discuss and illustrate' and Advanced level students generally find these the most difficult of all to tackle, since no clue is provided in the wording to suggest the course they should pursue. Many candidates think of a discussion as taking place between two or more people and feel bewildered and uncertain when expected to undertake this single-handed. All their puzzlement and doubt would probably disappear on the spot if they were told that 'Discuss' in this context means only 'Say what you think about . . . .' and 'illustrate' means 'produce evidence from the text either by quotation or by reference to support your opinion'. (Incredible as it may seem I have in the course of my thirty-six years' examining more than once received 'illustrated' scripts, i.e. with drawings of scenes and characters attached.)

These questions then really come under the heading of those demanding an expression of personal opinion and all that has been said in that section also applies to them. Candidates are being invited to say what they honestly think about some aspect of an author's work and there is no need for them to pretend to an admiration they do not feel, provided they can give substantial support to their unfavourable opinion by reference to or quotation from the text.

QUESTIONS FOR ADVANCED EXAMINATIONS

MISCELLANY ONE AND MISCELLANY TWO

QUESTION

'The obscurity of Dylan Thomas's poetry is not due to a lack of meaning. At times it has too many possible meanings.' Discuss and illustrate.

ANSWER

It is true that very often it is possible to interpret some of the most obscure lines in Thomas's poems in more than one way and, in that sense, his poetry may be said to have too many possible meanings. But if, when we have with great difficulty worked out these interpretations, we find them, for the most part, to be uninteresting and unilluminating then we can only condemn the line or verse for being of such insignificance, whichever way we work it out, that the time spent on elucidating it has been wasted.

Dylan Thomas has been dead long enough for various critical works to have been written about him. Very rarely do the critics agree on his meaning; they each do the best they can to interpret his poems and obviously they must have felt some admiration for him before embarking upon their studies but it seems to be the sound of his words that they admire rather than their sense. All of them lament his obscurity and we feel that our own guesses at what he means are just as likely to hit the mark as theirs. One might sometimes add 'if he means anything'. Occasionally one cannot help wondering if he is playing some enormous trick on his readers and seeing how much they will swallow.

Of course there are some poems which are wholly or largely intelligible and for obvious reasons these have become the most popular with his readers. The poem written as his father dies, 'Do not go gentle into that good night' is an example of these. It is perfectly clear that his father is submitting passively to death and that the poet cannot bear to see him so uncharacteristically gentle, quiet and subdued. He does not believe that death should be accepted but passionately resisted. 'Old age should burn and rave at close of day.' The imagery in this poem is both more beautiful and more understandable than in most of his work, 'their words had forked no lightning' and 'Blind eyes could gaze like meteors and be gay' are not too difficult to puzzle out and are certainly not repulsive as is much of his imagery.

'Fern Hill' is another comparatively easy poem to understand and it has a sunny, carefree, fresh atmosphere which we very rarely encounter in Thomas's poetry. He is writing of his childhood when he was 'young and easy under the apple boughs' and the poem is full of the enchanted feeling of the child's world. All the sun it was running, it was lovely'; the hay to him seems as high as the house; animals of all kinds surround him, as they surrounded Adam and Eve in Paradise; horses, foxes, pheasants, lambs, owls, the farmyard cock — all contribute to his happiness in his 'green and golden world' where everything, even the calves, seems to be singing for pure joy. Even if every single word and phrase is not crystal clear (for example the reference to 'riding to sleep'), the meaning of the whole poem is apparent and, moreover, it is a pleasant, enjoyable poem free from all his images of death and decay and symptoms of physical illness.

'Poem in October' has many of the same qualities as 'Fern Hill' and most of what has been said about that poem is applicable to this. 'A Springful of Larks', 'a wonder of summer with apples, peas and redcurrants', are phrases which conjure up happy memories and again there is nothing repellent in the poem.

A few other such poems are to be found in the Selections but the greater part of Thomas's verse chosen for inclusion here is of a very different kind. Perhaps the most striking example of these poems is 'I, in my intricate image' where, as is so often the case, Thomas's eyes are turned inwards on himself with apparent fascination. This poem is divided into three parts and even to find any evident connection between these is by no means simple. He seems to be examining two different facets of his personality but, as we struggle through verse after verse, we lose any continuous line of thought. The imagery here too is typical of Dylan Thomas, who is devoted to death and all its physical manifestations. What are we to make of 'Death instrumental Splitting the long eye open, and the spiral turnkey, Your corkscrew grave centred in navel and nipple' or 'The cadaverous gravels'? He is as fond of blood as of death and we feel almost cheated if he doesn't use the word once in a whole poem but so often he apparently uses it just because he likes it and not for its sense, as in '. . . blood and bubble casts to the pine roots'. We can see, as image succeeds image, that the poet is presenting the same thought to us in different ways but is it a thought worth presenting and worth our taking so much trouble to puzzle it out?

We may ask ourselves this question when we read 'I dreamt my genesis', by no means one of the most obscure poems set. In this poem, as in many others Thomas uses a technique peculiar to himself. At the same time as he develops his theme he is reminding us of something quite different by what may be called his 'stepping-stone' method. In line 2 he uses 'rotating', in line 3 'motor' and 'drill', in the second verse 'filed' and 'irons' and 'metal', in the third verse 'in bottom gear' and later 'blades', so that behind what he is actually saying, we are dimly aware of this factory image of great machines throbbing and pulsing and metal all around us and we realize that it cannot be by chance that Thomas so often employs this technique. He must for some reason want us to have a background to the message he is actually expressing in the fore-ground. However, far from making his poems easier to understand, it adds an additional complication. Possibly whoever formulated this question was thinking of this as one of the 'too many possible meanings'.

Some of Thomas's verses are capable of being interpreted in more than one way, perhaps in many ways. To take, for example, the first verse of 'I fellowed sleep'. Even the title is perplexing, since the ear expects 'I fell asleep', and 'followed' seems more likely, if we are to have a different phrase, than 'fellowed'. Presumably 'fellowed' here means 'treated as a friend', 'was in fellowship with', so, having reached this stage of elucidation, we expect the poem to tell of the poet's relationship with sleep, perhaps his longing for sleep as he might long for an absent friend. It is with this supposition in mind that we examine the first verse. 'Kissed' in the first line supports our theory of affectionate friendship, but there we leave sleep, which is not mentioned again in the whole poem, though the poet is apparently recounting a dream. He, himself, must be the 'sleeper' referred to in the second line and it seems that, in sleep, one aspect of himself is able to gaze at another, much as Marvell's soul, on the branch of the tree, looked down at Marvell, who looked up at him. It is the remaining lines of the verse which are capable of various explanations. 'So, planing-heeled, I flew along my man And dropped on dreaming and the upward sky'. This may mean that one facet of the poet is glancing quickly from one end of the sleeping man (himself) to the other and then splits off, as it were, from that part of the poet which was unconscious in bed and proceeds upwards to 'a second ground far from the stars', where it continues its own dream-life, unencumbered by the body. All students of metaphysical poetry are accustomed to this sort of experience and, with a little effort, we can persuade ourselves that this is the poet's meaning here. But Dylan Thomas was not conspicuously a metaphysical poet and he may have intended no such meaning. What is the significance of 'planing-heeled'? A plane is a carpenter's tool for smoothing rough wood. Is this line an image meaning 'I (the carpenter) ran my plane along my own body, smoothing off all its roughnesses (troubles and anxieties) and then, in a state of calm freedom from care, fell into a dream which took me up above the world's turmoil'?

We do not know which of these two meanings, if either, Thomas intended and if we had time we could probably work out various other interpretations. So, in this case, it may well be said that the poet has too many meanings or else, as was suggested earlier, no particular meaning at all.

Anyone who has heard a record of Dylan Thomas reading his

own poems will know that he gave tremendous stress to their sound value and read them, not to make the sense clear to his hearers, but to produce, with his gloriously rich voice, a unique quality of sound; not Milton's organ-music or the birdsong of some of the Romantic poets but a sound peculiarly his own, sonorous, magnificent, spell-binding. Is it not possible that it was to achieve this effect that he was really working and that the literal meaning of the words he employed was comparatively unimportant? Swinburne has often been accused of sacrificing sense to sound. May not Dylan Thomas's poetry show an even more exaggerated version of this defect, and the truth be, not that there are too many meanings in his lines but not enough?

QUESTION

'Dylan Thomas writes about common things in a most uncommon way.' Discuss and illustrate.

ANSWER

A frivolous way of beginning this essay would be to say that Thomas's poetry is so difficult to understand that we don't know whether he is writing about common things or not. A study of the index is not really helpful. 'I fellowed sleep' and 'I dreamed my genesis' and 'The force that through the green fuse drives the flower' are not simple titles and it is difficult to judge from them what the poems which begin in these ways are about. However, a closer look as the names of his poems does show us that he is preoccupied with certain matters and returns to them over and over again.

The most striking of these, perhaps, is Death. We find 'And death shall have no dominion over him', 'Elegy', 'After the funeral', 'A refusal to mourn the Death by Fire, of a Child in London', 'Deaths and Entrances', and we know that the 'Good night' into which he begs his father not to go 'gentle' stands for death too. This is a very large proportion of the total number of poems in the Selections and if Death can be called a common thing, he certainly writes a great deal about it.

It is necessary to examine some of the poems to decide whether Thomas treats this subject 'in a most uncommon way'. The simplest of all these poems is probably the one he wrote as his father was dying. He hates to see this man, once so full of life and spirit, submitting so passively at the end and begs him to fight and struggle every inch of the way. This view of death is surely not usual. Most of us hope that, when they die, those we love will suffer as little as possible. A peaceful death seems desirable both for ourselves and our friends and we should find it intensely distressing to sit by the bedside of a loved one and watch him fighting to live, prolonging the agony. So here the poet does take an uncommon view. The very title 'A Refusal to Mourn for the Death, by Fire, of a Child in London' is strange. The death of any child seems particularly sad and even complete strangers feel compassion for parents who have lost a child and might well mourn with them. If Dylan Thomas were basing his refusal to mourn on the Christian certainty that the child was not in fact dead but had passed into eternal life and was happier than she had been on earth, we could at least understand what might seem a fanatically religious point of view, but this is not apparently the case. The poem is full of obscurities, such as 'And I must enter again The round Zion of the water bead' and it is far from easy to discover exactly what it is upon which he is basing his refusal. The last line of the poem certainly suggests the possibility that the child may have gone to some sort of heaven, though it may also be interpreted as her total annihilation, but the rest of the poem does not seem to be inspired by Christian feeling. In the third verse Thomas visualizes the child's burning as some magnificent spectacle, 'The majesty and burning of the child's death', and he goes on to say that any lament for her innocence and youth would be a blasphemy. He leaves us with a picture of her returned to her Mother Earth, 'Secret by the unmourning water of the riding Thames'. All this strikes us as an extraordinary way to look at the death of a child.

Probably, of all the poems about Death, 'And Death shall have no dominion' is the most conventional in thought. The title is optimistic and cheering and this same note of confidence in Death's incapacity to prevail runs through every verse. 'Though lovers be lost love shall not', 'Strapped to a wheel, yet they shall not break'; these are encouraging strengthening lines, which have far more in common with other poets' attitudes to death than most of Dylan Thomas's work.

But it is not only Thomas's viewpoint on Death which is unusual but also his manner of expressing himself. The poems so far referred to are among the simplest in the Selections but even in these there are lines which cause us to stop and ponder over their meaning. 'After the funeral' is not nearly so straightforward. We hear of a desolate boy 'who slits his throat in the dark of the coffin and sheds dry leaves, That breaks one bone to light with a judgment clout'. No one could possibly argue that this is a common way of writing about death. His imagery, too, is often pre-

70

occupied with the subject of Death and in this aspect of his work we see the same departure from a 'common way' of writing. The last two lines of 'Do you not father' present an image of death. 'Love's house, they answer, and the tower death Lie all unknowing of the grave sin-eater', but these lines have to be read and re-read before the meaning is apparent. In 'I, in my intricate image', much more death imagery is used, for example, 'Death instrumental, Splitting the long eye open, and the spiral turnkey, Your corkscrew grave centred in navel and nipple . . .' but what precisely it all means is anybody's guess. We know that Thomas often gives us a picture of an eye being pierced, perhaps this has some special meaning for him which is lost upon us but, even if this is so, it does not make his verse any more comprehensible or 'common'.

Death figures as prominently in Thomas's prose as in his verse and here, too, it is very often death by drowning, and there is the same confusion as is so often seen in the poetry between Death and Life. 'Dead alive, drowned, raised up.' He continues, too, to show in his prose his old obsession with the worms that devour the dead, 'Now the worm and the death-beetle undid the fibres of the animal bones'. Indeed, every point that has been made about Death in his poetry is valid for his prose too.

Sex is another of his chief preoccupations, presumably a 'common thing', and Birth, which follows naturally from the sexual act.

'From love's first fever' is one of the poems which show this very clearly. Such words as 'womb', 'caul', 'breast', 'stream of milk' are all connected with the birth and early life of a baby and at the end of the poem that baby has become a man with a sex life of his own. 'I learnt the verbs of will and had my secret'. The very title, 'I dreamed my genesis' and such lines as 'Heir to the scalding veins that hold love's drop' are further evidence of his absorption in sex and much of his imagery is derived from this source.

This is equally evident in his prose. 'The Mouse and the Woman' is full of sex; so are 'The Map of Love' and 'A Prophet of the Sea'. Not only does he use sexual material for his subject matter, but, as always, he draws his imagery from it and sometimes startles us with the opposite of what we expect. In 'The Mouse and the Woman' he writes 'She had moved in his belly when he was a boy, and stirred in his boy's loins'.

There are many other examples of his unusual approach to this subject, his writing of it in an uncommon way. The whole of 'The Map of Love' bears the imprint of his hand and could not be mistaken by anybody who knows his work for that of any other writer. This account of how 'Mad Jarvis . . . . had sown his seed in the belly of a bald headed girl' is far from the romantic attitude towards physical love so often adopted.

So, by considering Thomas's treatment of Death, Sex and Birth surely three of the most universal experiences of life, and by showing his unusual approach to them and particularly the unusual language he employs to describe them, it has been established that the saying quoted in the title is a true one. One might go even further and say that Thomas writes of these and other matters in a unique way which makes his work stand out distinctly from that of any other poet.

THE NEW MEN

QUESTION

Discuss the different moral attitudes taken by the characters towards (1) the making and (2) the using of the nuclear bomb in *The New Men*.

ANSWER

During the course of *The New Men* we see some of the characters engaged in weighing grave moral issues, one against another, in an attempt to decide whether it is defensible to try to make the nuclear bomb at all. At first there is no thought in anyone's mind of using it; it is envisaged simply as a deterrent of such magnitude that its possession, once made known to the enemy, will be certain to bring the war to an end. Looked at in this way it will be a means to saving countless lives and preventing damage to homes, cities and valuables of all kinds. Naturally there are those who argue fervently for the work on the bomb to continue, if it will bring about the immediate end of hostilities. Yet some feel that even with such a worthy end in view, it is morally indefensible to create a weapon capable of laying waste a large town and killing or cruelly maiming nearly all its inhabitants.

Not every character can view the moral issue without being distracted by personal considerations — the brothers Lewis and Martin Eliot are two of these. During the course of the book we are made aware that Lewis is, as it were, trying to live his life again through his younger brother, as some fathers do through their sons. He is more ambitious for Martin than he is for himself, more delighted by his success, more grieved by his failures. Martin, too, longs for recognition as a scientist; to make a name for himself, but no doubt he has realized, as Lewis has, that though he is

72

clever, he is not clever enough to reach the top. When Martin asks his brother to get him into Barford, the scientific establishment at which the work on the nuclear bomb is to be done, and Lewis realizes that this may possibly give Martin his last chance of eminence in the world of science, it is impossible that either brother can view the moral problem involved in making the bomb without having his opinion coloured by his desires and hopes. Neither of them is in any ignorance of the potentially destructive nature of the weapon planned; very early in the story Bevill describes its effect as being 'like thousands of tons of T.N.T.' and he makes it clear to Lewis in this conversation that 'whichever side got the weapon first would win the war' but he does not mean by using the weapon; that has not yet entered anyone's mind.

The news that the Germans are also working on the bomb puts new strength into the arguments of those who are advocating it in England. At this stage Lewis says frankly, 'I did not believe that anything would come of it, and my chief interest was that it might give Martin a better chance', making it plain that, as he has not even recognized the possibilities of success, there is really as yet no moral problem for him. Martin, by his eagerness to work at Barford, shows that he feels the same way. The research may not succeed; if it does it will stop the war and that must be good.

Up to now only Francis Getliffe has had the perception to see further and to say uncompromisingly' I hope it's *never* possible'.

It is very difficult to spare first-class scientists to work at Barford and the place is largely staffed by refugees like the Puchweins who no doubt delight in being able to use their scientific knowledge and training in any way that the country which has offered them asylum demands of them and they do not seem to have been torn by doubts and scruples as some of their English colleagues later are.

At first two different lines of research are going on simultaneously at Barford and Martin begins working there under Rudd but later transfers to Luke's section. Luke himself is a passionate believer in the possibility of success, a brilliant and inspiring man who, like many of his kind, seeks only to enlarge the bounds of knowledge for mankind and, absorbed in the interest of his work, does not agonize over the moral issues connected with it.

Drawbell, at the head of the establishment, is a religious man who thinks deeply. 'I pray God that my people here will get it first. Pray God we get it.' This may mean simply that getting it first means winning the war but it seems possible by the fervency of his prayer that Drawbell has envisaged the possibility that if the Germans get it first, they may use it.

The establishment at Barford has its ups and downs and at one time there is an idea of closing it down and sending off the English scientists to work with the Americans but nothing comes of this and the research goes on. It is while Lewis is dining with Bevill at Pratts that the question is raised of what will actually be done with the bomb, once it is made. Most of the scientists have agreed that a notification to the enemy that England has a bomb will be enough to stop the war. Bevill is not sure. 'I wonder', he says, 'has there ever been a weapon that someone did not want to let off?' Lewis's view is that this bomb is so different in kind from any other weapon that its usage would be unthinkable but Bevill is not convinced.

Some time later Lewis quotes what Bevill said to Martin and Mounteney, who stress the appalling damage the bomb would do. Martin is insistent that it must never be used; Lewis secretly wonders whether the Germans would not use it if they got it first. None of the three sees this problem except as one which may arise in the future but Lewis has to admit he finds it *almost* incredible that anyone would drop the bomb. Martin declares 'I think it is incredible'. All three agree that people must be taught just what its effects would be, to make perfectly sure it is never used.

The first test at Barford proves a failure causing Mary Pearson to sob, Sawbridge, the spy, to be sufficiently moved almost to follow her example and everyone else concerned to feel a sickening disappointment, which pushes further into the future the question of using the bomb if it were ever made and Lewis persuades Sir Hector Rose to let the scientists try again.

Then espionage complicates the story when Captain Smith comes to investigate how information about the nuclear research has been leaked. He suspects Sawbridge and Lewis asks Martin if he 'could imagine him fanatical enough to give secrets away'. Nobody, it seems, thinks Sawbridge's concern is money; he is presumably motivated by the passionate concern of many scientists that knowledge should not be hoarded but made universally available — a viewpoint which Martin shares and which makes him hate the necessity in wartime of keeping results of experiments secret. Mounteney feels the same — 'Science belongs to mankind'.

The next test is a success but not before another moral problem has arisen over the making of the bomb. Luke and Sawbridge become very ill as a result of their work on it, the former critically. Who is to be asked to risk his health, perhaps his life, in continuing the research? Martin, who is terrified, nevertheless volunteers and seems the obvious choice.

Then Pearson, who has been sent over to the USA to work with the American scientists arrives with the news that they have made some bombs and one is to be dropped in the desert to discover 'if it goes off all right'. The question looms hugely of what will be done with the other bombs.

The test in North Mexico is a complete success and Getliffe tells Lewis of his fears that the Americans will be tempted to drop the bomb. By now all thought of using it solely as a deterrent seems to have receded into the remote past. Lewis and Getliffe are summoned to Barford for a conference, Getliffe still repeating 'They can't drop the bomb'. His reasons are not only moral but practical. Within five years all the major powers will have the bomb. 'If we dropped them first — .'

At the conference some of the scientists positively veto the use of the bomb; others are almost as definitely against it, believing that the feeling of guilt such an abominable action would leave, would never fade. Most of them are against its use but would agree to it, if it were the only way to stop the war. This is Luke's view and Getliffe has apparently weakened enough to go along with it. He says that in America those who argued for using the bomb were saying that Japan must be invaded and if the use of the bomb would save human lives, it must be used. No other motive for using it was thinkable for civilized people. Getliffe continues that he is in favour of a three-pronged operation; first to tell the enemy they have the bomb, then to drop one where no human life is at stake and only then, if the enemy refuses to yield, to drop one on a town. Everyone points out that the Official Secrets Act would make this impossible and it is finally agreed that two or three English scientists should go to America taking a petition signed by as many people concerned as possible against dropping the bomb on a city. Before they can carry out this plan the first bomb is dropped. Lewis feels there is no more they can do. 'I disagree', says Martin.

His first idea is to write a letter to *The Times* pointing out that the Allies have perpetrated the most horrible single act so far performed. With great difficulty he is persuaded not to send it but this ambitious man, so proud of his achievements up to date, finds the moral strength to refuse the high appointment (and no doubt, in course of time, the knighthood) which now lies within his grasp, because he cannot continue to work in defiance of his principles, no matter what the material rewards. Possibly he is influenced in his decision by the horrifying story he relates so drily to his brother. Before the bomb was dropped it was suggested that a huge flare should be set off in the sky, the object of this being to ensure that everyone would be looking up, and so no one could escape being blinded when the real bomb dropped a moment later.

It is depressing to see as we follow the change in moral attitudes throughout the course of the story that only Martin sacrifices anything for his beliefs. He has changed as a result of knowing that the bomb has been used and can be used again. When he first began working at Barford he was not even sure that it could ever be made and nobody at that time really considered its use a possibility. The others, on the whole, have weakened in their moral attitudes, even Getliffe who at the beginning is against any work on the bomb at all. Strangely enough it is Sawbridge who gives up most for his conviction that scientific knowledge should be common property. C.P. Snow shows us powerfully how circumstances erode a man's finer beliefs and ideals until, imperceptibly, he sinks far below his own former standards.

SUMMING-UP

You have already been told more than once in this book to say what you really think, if given the chance, even if it is not what you believe is the generally accepted view. The first examination answers in this section are fairly predictable but the advanced level answers are more daring and find plenty to criticize in C.P. Snow's novel and Dylan Thomas's poetry. Since all the unfavourable comments are supported by illustrations from the texts (for instance, examples are given of Snow's unilluminating images and Thomas's obscurity and so forth) they are no less likely to gain good marks than lavish praise would be. The important thing, as all these answers show, is to make clear what has led to your opinion, whether it is favourable or unfavourable.

8 Miscellaneous Questions

INTRODUCTION

There are always some questions which do not fit precisely into any category. The candidate who has practised writing answers to the various types of question which appear regularly in the Literature papers will be unlikely to find any difficulty in dealing with most of these, which are usually extremely straightforward and self-explanatory.

One more exacting kind is that which requires a selection of information to be picked out from the book as a whole and candidates who do not regard themselves as 'high fliers' would be well advised to leave these and choose something less ambitious.

QUESTIONS FOR FIRST EXAMINATIONS

NORTHANGER ABBEY

EXPLANATORY NOTE

This novel, published in 1818, tells of Catherine Morland's visits, first to Bath with some kind friends of her parents, and then to stay at Northanger Abbey with the Tilney family, whom she meets there. There was a tremendous fashion at this time for mysterious, romantic novels in which the action often took place in ruined, ivy-covered castles or abbeys, most of it generally by moonlight, and innocent maidens were very much at risk from dishonourable seducers, while inconvenient wives, long believed by the world to be dead, were, in fact, actually imprisoned by their vile husbands, who had to feed them secretly at night. Catherine has been greatly influenced by this kind of reading and expects Northanger Abbey to be very different from what, in fact, she finds. However, she does have a very disagreeable experience there and has to undergo considerable suffering before, at the end of the book, she is happily married to Henry Tilney.

QUESTION

What do we learn from **Northanger Abbey** of the social life of the time?

For a hundred years, covering the period in which Jane Austen wrote, Bath vied with London as the centre of the fashionable world and its activities. Between them the architect Wood and Beau Nash, for so long the autocratic Master of Ceremonies, created a unique setting for the entertainments and amusements of the leisured rich. No description is given in the novel of the social pleasures offered by London at this time, but Catherine Morland's visit to Bath and the opportunities for enjoyment there are fully described.

Catherine was one of the ten children of a country clergyman and her social life, apart from her visit to Bath, was of the simplest. There must obviously have been a friendly interchange of visits with neighbouring families, since the Allens had become sufficiently fond of Catherine to take her to Bath with them. But 'the chaise of a traveller' was 'a rare sight in Fullerton', so much so that at the first glimpse of one, 'the whole family were immediately at the window'. Evidently the circle of acquaintances was very restricted. Soon after Catherine's return home from the Abbey she and her mother walked together to pay a call on the Allens, and Henry Tilney and Catherine set off, with the same object in view, shortly after his arrival at Fullerton. Catherine's day spent at Woodston, in spite of its simplicity, with its 'saunter' into the meadows, its visit to the stables and the 'charming game' with the puppies, was a very satisfactory one.

Longer visits to stay with friends were also a regular part of the social life of the time. Catherine was invited to Northanger Abbey and General Tilney made a suddenly recollected visit to Lord Longtown's, near Hereford, his excuse for expelling her from his home.

But it is at Bath that we see the social life of the time at its glittering height. Every form of entertainment then in vogue could be enjoyed there in the most elegant of surroundings and with the most cultivated, wealthy, and fashionable companions. The Pump-room, where the Spa water could be taken, was the centre where all sought each other out and signed their names in the Pump-room book, adding their temporary addresses so that friends, both old and new could discover them in their apartments. Catherine, like all the rest, was there every day and sometimes 'the crowd was insupportable'; on other occasions she and Isabella were able to hold an intimate conversation without interruption.

Balls, a great feature of the social life of Bath, were held in the Assembly Rooms. Strictly chaperoned, the girls sat awaiting partners and watching those fortunate enough to be already taking part in the various sets scattered over the floor. Country-dancing followed the more formal cotillions and in these partners were separated for a great part of each dance. Meanwhile, in the card room, those gentlemen who did not care for dancing were enjoying themselves at the table.

The theatre was another popular form of entertainment and some, at least, of the audience seemed to spend almost as much time watching each other as the play. Certainly Isabella cannot have seen much of the performance from her box as we are told she 'talked the rest of the evening to James'. Henry Tilney, on the other hand, atoned for a previously professed lack of interest in the theatre on the night when, offended by Catherine's behaviour, 'his notice was never withdrawn from the stage for two whole scenes'.

The calls which Catherine was used to in Fullerton were far more exciting and stimulating in Bath, where new friends and acquaintances constantly visited each other in their lodgings. Although Catherine's first visit to the Tilneys in Milsom Street ended in humiliation for her, the next produced an invitation to dine and spend the day there.

Walks to some neighbouring beauty spot were another enjoyable way of passing the time, though 'a few specks of small rain' were enough to threaten such a plan. Sometimes the gentlemen went riding together; Henry Tilney accompanied his father on one such occasion. A more dashing kind of outdoor entertainment was to drive to some place of interest. The perfidious Thorpe set out with Catherine to Blaize Castle, her brother riding behind, but he had misjudged the distance and they were forced to turn back before their objective was reached.

It is debatable whether long conversations about people and books would today be considered to be a feature of social life but there is no doubt that Jane Austen presents them in this light. People evidently talked and discussed far more than they do today, possibly because there was no radio or television as a substitute. The girls, Catherine and Isabella, were engrossed in reading *The Mysteries of Udolpho* and loved comparing notes on the book as well as on all that was going on around them and Henry and Catherine had much to say to each other about novels on the walk to Beechen Cliff. There was time for this sort of pleasure then and in this way people were able to get to know each other gradually and thoroughly.

Jane Austen gives us a convincing picture of the interest and gaiety and excitement of life in Bath and leaves us in no doubt

that what might seem an intolerably restricted and dull pro-
gramme to the young people of today, provided for the privileged
youth of her own time some thrilling and sometimes breath-
takingly enjoyable experiences.

'MORTE D'ARTHUR'

EXPLANATORY NOTE

This poem is the last of the collection of poems by Tennyson called *The
Idylls of the King*, which deal with the life of King Arthur, from the time of
his arrival on this earth, of which there are various versions, till his strange
end. His greatest feats were to unite the warring peoples of this country and
then, by the institution of The Round Table and with the help of his noble
knights, to keep the peace and to continue to fight against evil of all kinds in
defence of the right. Sadly, there was a traitor at his court who infected
others to rebel against him and his dearest and most trusted friend, Sir
Lancelot, proved false to him and made love to his Queen, Guinevere. A
battle took place 'in the West' between King Arthur and those loyal to him
and the rebellious knights, and the King was fatally injured. Sir Bedivere
is the last of all the knights, the others all having been killed, and he stays
loyally alone with the dying king until he is mysteriously transported out of
sight on a black-draped barge, escorted by three queens.

These words are spoken by Arthur to Bedivere shortly before his departure.

QUESTION

Ah! my Lord Arthur, Whither shall I go?
Where shall I hide my forehead and my eyes?
For now I see the true old times are dead,
When every morning brought a noble chance,
And every chance brought out a noble knight.
Such times have been not since the light that led
The Holy Elders with the gift of myrrh.

(i)   What was the event that had brought the 'old times' to an
      end?
(ii) Explain the fourth and fifth lines.
(iii) Why does Sir Bedivere compare the Round Table with 'the
      light that led the Holy Elders with the gift of myrrh?'
(iv) How in his reply does King Arthur reassure Sir Bedivere
      about the future?

ANSWER

(i)   The last battle in the West where Arthur's knights had 'fallen in Lyonesse about their lord', fighting for him against the disloyal Knights of the Round Table.

(ii) Every morning at Arthur's court those people who were suffering from some injustice or oppression and who needed help in righting their wrongs presented themselves to the King. If he considered their case worthy of his support he would detail a knight to go and fight for them.

(iii) All through the story of Arthur, there is a faint parallel with the life of Christ. Both of them came into the world in an unusual way and neither of them died in the normal sense but, having been killed by those they had tried to help, went away for a time in order to come again at some later date. Therefore some imagery from the Bible seems quite suitable.

In this case, just as the star in the East led the Wise Men to their infant Saviour, so the Round Table had shone, in its goodness and purity, through the wicked world surrounding it and had led those in trouble to make their way towards it to ask help from Arthur who would save them.

(iv) Arthur replies that change must come and God shows His greatness in every new development. He tells Bedivere he must find comfort within himself, 'no comfort is in me'. He asks the knight to pray for him. 'More things are wrought by prayer than this world dreams of." Men are no better than sheep or goats, if, knowing God, they fail to pray to him for themselves and for their friends.

'For so the whole round earth is every way
Bound by gold chains about the feet of God.'

Finally he tells Bedivere that he is not going to die but is to be taken 'to the island Valley of Avilion', a place like Paradise, where he will be healed of 'his grievous wound'.

'THE RIME OF THE ANCIENT MARINER'

EXPLANATORY NOTE

The Ancient Mariner, in Coleridge's poem, brings bad luck to his ship and fellow-sailors by killing an albatross and, as a punishment, he feels a compulsion from time to time to tell the story of all the strange consequences which followed upon his act. This question deals with one of the horrifying experiences which befell him.

QUESTION

Illustrating your answer by quotations from or close reference to

the poem, give an account of the experiences of the Ancient
Mariner when his ship was becalmed on the Equator.

ANSWER

After shooting the Albatross, the Mariner had been first blamed
and then praised by his fellow-seamen according to whether his
action seemed to have brought them bad or good luck. As the ship
sailed merrily along before 'the fair breeze' all seemed to be well
but suddenly the ship 'burst' into a 'silent sea' and from that
moment the real suffering of the Mariner and his companions
began.

Immediately the breeze dropped 'the sails dropt down' and an
unearthly silence made the men chatter to each other just 'to
break the silence of the sea'.

Right over the mast at mid-day 'the bloody sun' shone in the
'hot and copper sky' and 'day after day' the ship lay motionless,
'as idle as a painted ship upon a painted ocean'. Now the men
became tortured by thirst. All around them lay the water, yet the
boards of the deck were warping with dryness and they had not
'any drop to drink'.

As the Mariner gazed down at the sea, it seemed to him that
'the very deep did rot' and he hated the 'slimy things' which
crawled 'with legs upon the slimy sea'. At night he saw marvellous
colour effects when 'the death-fires danced' and the water seemed
to him 'green, and blue, and white', 'like a witch's oils'. Some of
the mariners had horrible dreams about the spirit which was
causing their distress. It had followed them all the way from the
South Pole, 'nine fathom deep' below the boat, to gain revenge for
the slaughtered Albatross. But soon they could no longer tell of
their dreams for 'every tongue through utter drought was withered
at the root'. Then, of course, all the seamen regarded the Mariner
with 'evil looks' and they took away the cross which hung around
his neck and hung the Albatross there instead.

Time dragged by and the men's eyes became glassy. Suddenly
the Mariner spotted in the west a speck moving towards them.
Next it seemed a mist but finally he recognized it as a ship which
'as if it dodged a water sprite' came plunging and tacking and
veering in their direction. Unable to warn his companions in any
other way, the Mariner had to bite his arm and suck the blood to
moisten his lips enough to cry, 'A sail! A sail!' Open-mouthed they
heard him and managed to grin, as they gasped for air.

But the ship soon terrified them. It came towards them 'without a breeze, without a tide' and as it was outlined against the

'broad bright sun', which was just sinking into 'the western wave', it made it look as if the sun was peering through prison bars. Soon the Mariner could see that it was only a skeleton ship, with sails 'like restless gossameres' and that it was manned by a horrible crew of two, a woman and a skeleton. The woman looked repulsive, 'her lips were red, her looks were free, her locks were yellow as gold; Her skin was as white as leprosy'. She was the 'Nightmare Life-in-Death' who makes men's blood run cold with terror.

As the ship came alongside, the Mariner saw that the two were playing at dice and with a threefold whistle, the woman cried out that she had won her throw for the life of the Mariner. Suddenly 'at one stride' it was dark and the little boat shot away. Then as the stars shone and the 'horrid moon' rose, each of the 200 men on board 'turned his face with a ghastly pang' to the Mariner and 'cursed' him 'with his eye', as they dropped lifeless upon the deck. As each one died his soul passed by the Ancient Mariner 'like the whizz of my cross-bow'.

Then began an appalling time for the Mariner. He was 'alone alone, all, all alone, Alone on a wide wide sea', with only the 'slimy things' and the dead bodies to keep him company. He could not pray and he could not escape the last looks of the dead men, who did not 'rot nor reek'. A whole week of this torture passed and he watched the moon whose frosty light was cast over the 'still and awful red' of the sea. Suddenly he realized how beautiful the water-snakes were with their glorious colours and a feeling of love for their happiness and beauty arose in his heart 'and he blessed them unaware'. At that moment the spell began to lose its force, he found he could pray and,

'The Albatross fell off and sank
Like lead into the sea'.

At last he could sleep and he dreamed that the ship's buckets 'were filled with dew'. When he woke up it was raining. He was quite light headed and wondered if he had died. Then the extraordinary storm began, with 'rivers' of lightning and wind and rain and the ship began to move. The dead men rose to man her and the period of total calm was at an end.

JULIUS CAESAR

QUESTION

Write on two of the following as they affect the development of the play, referring closely to relevant scenes. (a) Dreams, auguries and portents; (b) The attitude of the citizens of Rome to those in power; (c) The cleverness of Antony.

ANSWER

(a)

Calphurnia's dream on the night before Caesar's assassination could have saved her husband's life. Caesar tells Decius that she had dreamt that she saw his 'statua', spouting 'pure blood' like a fountain, out of a hundred spouts. Many 'lusty' Romans ran to bathe their hands in it, smiling all the time. Calphurnia was very much frightened by this dream which she regarded as a warning of some forthcoming disaster to her husband and she had made him promise to stay at home that day. If only Caesar had kept his promise, he would probably not have been murdered. However Decius interprets the dream in a way very flattering to Caesar, explaining that it signified that 'from you great Rome shall suck reviving blood' and thus he persuades Caesar to go to his death.

A dream is mentioned on another occasion in Brutus's tent, when Lucius falls asleep playing his instrument. While he sleeps the ghost of Caesar appears to his master and Lucius must have been partly conscious of this supernatural happening for, after the ghost's disappearance, Brutus asks him 'Didst thou dream, Lucius, that thou so criedst out?' but Lucius assures him he did not know he had cried out and he had not seen anything.

The augurers are only mentioned once in the play by that name, on the morning of Caesar's murder. Caesar asks his servant what they have foretold and the servant tells him that he should not leave the house that day because 'Plucking the entrails of an offering forth, They could not find a heart within the beast'. Although Caesar has been sufficiently interested to ask for the augurers' opinion, he disregards it when he gets it, declaring 'Caesar should be a beast without a heart if he should stay at home today for fear'. If he had listened to them he might have been saved.

The Soothsayer also foretells Caesar's death and tries to warn him. Just before Caesar goes to watch the Lupercal Games, the Soothsayer approaches him in the street and cries 'Beware the Ides of March' but Caesar dismisses him as a dreamer. Again on the morning of Caesar's assassination the Soothsayer tells Portia he is going to give Caesar another warning, which he does, telling him that the Ides of March are not yet over but again Caesar refuses to listen and so moves on to his death.

Portents occur very frequently in the play. Immediately after the conspirators' plan has been made Rome is troubled by a violent thunder storm which seems to the people to be beyond any normal storm. 'Never till tonight, never till now' says Casca, 'Did I go through a tempest dropping fire', and he wonders whether the Gods intend thus to destroy the people.

Casca has many other strange happenings to report to Cicero; a slave held up his flaming left hand which remained undestroyed; a lion glared at him near the Capitol; a hundred terrified women swore they had seen 'men all in fire walk up and down the streets'; the owl had hooted at mid-day in the market-place − all these things were regarded as 'portentous'.

When Cassius joins them he speaks of 'gliding ghosts' and tells how 'there is no stir or walking in the streets' because of these happenings.

Calphurnia tells Caesar of other 'horrid sights seen by the watch'. A lioness 'hath whelped in the streets', the dead have risen from their graves, armies have fought in the clouds and 'drizzled blood upon the Capitol' and the ghosts this time are spoken of as shrieking and squealing about the streets.

All these supernatural happenings lead the Romans to expect a major disaster and prepare them for the death of Caesar. They add to the atmosphere of the play and make it more exciting and thrilling.

(b)
We first see the citizens of Rome at the very beginning of the play when they have poured out into the streets, although it is not a public holiday, to greet Caesar 'who comes in triumph over Pompey's blood'. Flavius and Marullus, who are tribunes opposed to Caesar, point out to the people their contemptible fickleness, reminding them that only a short time ago they were waiting the 'live-long day in patient expectation to see great Pompey pass the streets of Rome'. Evidently the people do not care deeply who is in power, as long as they get their opportunities for enjoyment. They have decked the statues with scarves but 'vanish tongue-tied in their guiltiness' when the tribunes rebuke them.

We next hear of the crowd from Casca who tells how Mark Antony three times offered Caesar a crown. At first the crowd was delighted at Caesar's refusal and 'hooted and clapped their chapped hands' but after he had had a fit they were sentimentally ready to forgive him anything. In fact they are ruled entirely by their emotions, not their reasons, and are ready to support any ruler who makes an emotional appeal to them.

The most striking scene in which the crowd's reactions are

shown is that of Caesar's funeral. They are disturbed and shocked at Caesar's death and shout 'We will be satisfied, let us be satisfied'. Brutus makes a reasoned explanation to them (Shakespeare's use of prose here is masterly) of why they killed Caesar. 'Not that I loved Caesar less, but that I loved Rome more'. The crowd are prepared to accept his words but go much too far in their absurd volte-face, revealing that they have not really understood at all what Brutus meant by the necessity to stamp out Caesarism, when they shout 'Let him be Caesar!' and do their best to put Brutus in the dead Caesar's place.

They are in this mood when Antony begins to address them. Understanding them thoroughly, he appeals to their emotions, to their pity, to their greed, and stirs them up into a frenzy of mad hatred against the conspirators.

So we see the Roman people have no intelligent judgment of their rulers but sway with every wind and are prepared to applaud anyone who knows how to talk to them.

(c)
We first see Antony as an athlete competing in the Lupercal Games. We may not realize then how clever he is, and Caesar talks of him as 'Antony that revels long o'nights'. However there is far more to Antony than the sportsman and the reveller. It is not until the scene of Caesar's funeral that we first detect his cleverness in knowing how to deal with people.

He is set on having revenge. It is therefore obviously necessary for him to stay alive until he has carried out his purpose. So it is not lack of courage but cunning which makes him send his servant to the conspirators after Caesar's death to spy out the land before he ventures to appear himself. When he comes he has, as it were, to walk on a tight-rope between appearing to be an enemy to the conspirators on the one hand and appearing to be a most disloyal friend to Caesar on the other. The clever Antony manages this difficult task perfectly. He has already ascertained from his servant that it is perfectly safe for him to present himself before the conspirators but he puts on an act, pretending to be quite willing to die by the same sword and in the same hour as Caesar.

Brutus assures him that they intend him no harm and, continuing his clever act, Antony forces himself to shake hands with them all, though later he apologizes to Caesar's dead body that he was 'meek and gentle with these butchers'. He says 'friends am I with you all' and convinces Brutus at any rate.

Next he asks if he may speak at Caesar's funeral and in spite of Cassius's objections, Brutus agrees. We know Antony's true intentions from the soliloquy he utters over Caesar's body and the prophecy he makes of civil war in Italy, 'And Caesar's spirit ranging for revenge, With Ate by his side come hot from hell', but the conspirators do not realize how he really feels.

When Octavius Caesar's servant comes to Antony, Antony tells him to wait before returning to his master, until he can report how Antony's speech to the people has gone. When Antony begins speaking, the crowd is in favour of Brutus and Antony is careful at first to say nothing against the conspirators which might antagonize his hearers. 'For Brutus is an honourable man, so are they all, all honourable men' he declares but gradually as he repeats these phrases a more and more sarcastic note sounds through his words. He reminds his hearers of all Caesar has done for them and shows that he was plainly not ambitious, as Brutus has said. He has given his prisoners' ransoms to the 'general coffers' of Rome, he has refused the crown he was offered.

Knowing well the importance of rousing the crowd's emotions, he tells them he must pause while he conquers his own grief. 'My heart is in the coffin there with Caesar, And I must pause till it come back to me.' Already he is winning the crowd over, though he pretends that the last thing he wishes to do is 'to stir your hearts and minds to mutiny and rage'.

He next cunningly mentions Caesar's will but says he dares not read it to them because 'it will inflame you, it will make you mad', although he tantalizingly tells them they are 'Caesar's heirs'. They naturally clamour to hear more and he makes them stand round Caesar's corpse, so that he can the better appeal to their pity. He points out to them Caesar's mantle and tells them he wore it first at the battle in which he defeated the Nervii by his own extraordinary bravery. It is most unlikely that Antony would really know whether he wore the cloak on that day.

Next he points out to them all Caesar's wounds saying which one was made by each conspirator and nobody realizes that Antony had not even been present at the assassination and could not possibly have known this. In spite of his absence from the scene he gives a most moving account of Caesar's murder and has the crowd sobbing all round him and crying 'We will be revenged'.

In a speech which is a triumph of irony and deception Antony assures them with his tongue in his cheek that he does not want to stir them to mutiny and revenge, that he is 'no orator, As Brutus is', but the crowd are almost out of hand by now and he finds it quite difficult to calm them enough to hear the will, which they have by now forgotten about but which he, in spite of his protestations, has every intention of reading.

By the time he has finished telling them of what Caesar has left them, he has perfectly achieved his purpose and has manipulated the people into a state of mad hysteria, so that they tear to pieces Cinna the poet, just because he has the same name as one of the conspirators.

In the scene where Antony is attending to business matters with his fellow triumvirs, Octavius Caesar and Lepidus, we see a different kind of cleverness, a callous determination to get his own way, whoever suffers. He is willing for his sister's son to be killed if necessary and it is evident that now that Lepidus has served his purpose he has every intention of 'turning him off'. At the end of the scene it is Antony who takes the lead in considering how to wage the war against the conspirators.

We do not see much of Antony in the battle of Philippi but his side wins which suggests he is as clever in war as he is in politics. Certainly he is clever in his judgment of men for, in the generous tribute he pays to his dead enemy, Brutus, he recognizes that 'This was the noblest Roman of them all'.

NB All three parts of the question have been answered here, although only two are asked for.

QUESTIONS FOR ADVANCED EXAMINATIONS

THE NEW MEN

QUESTION

Give a description of the establishment at Barford and tell the story of its successes and failures.

ANSWER

We first hear about the nuclear research which is the theme of *The New Men* in a conversation which took place between Lewis Eliot, the Minister under whom he served during the war, Sir Thomas Bevill, and Sir Hector Rose, a top Civil Servant. None of these three was a scientist and the other two were incredulous when Bevill told them 'some of these scientists believe they can present us with a great big bang. Like thousands of tons of T.N.T.' and that the possession of this bomb would lead to the end of the Second World War. The project was to be referred to by the code name 'Mr Toad'.

For some time nothing was done about this plan but the news that the Germans were working on the bomb accelerated matters and by the Spring of 1941 permission had been granted for a small establishment to be set up at Barford in Warwickshire. It was extremely difficult to staff this centre and most of the scientists working there had to be refugees. Eventually Walter Luke and Lewis's brother Martin were also appointed to positions there and Martin began his employment at Barford in June.

Lewis paid his first visit to the establishment the following November and inspected the laboratories and listened to 'the clicking of Geiger counters' but could understand very little of what was going on. The next day he saw more of the set-up, situated on a disused airfield, bleak, unattractive, cold, half-derelict and the last place to inspire confidence as the centre of important scientific research. The house which Drawbell, the Supervisor, and his secretaries occupied was some way from the airfield along a country path. It had once been a fine house and Drawbell's office had been the main drawing-room, a very long room with a parquet floor and white panelling, now almost obliterated by charts and diagrams pinned up on it. His secretaries worked elsewhere in a fairly conventional office equipped with typewriters and dictaphones.

The place is described far more fully at the time of Lewis's visit in May 1943 when work had begun on the construction of the machine necessary for the manufacture of the bomb. The tar-paulins, still not repaired, flapped in the wind. It was still cold but the damp of his previous visit had given place to dry dust and grit. Everything looked messy and derelict. Workmen were en-gaged in building an outer wall for 'the pile', outside which was yet another wall, 'the first part of the concrete case'. A mysterious sort of box about 8ft x 8ft stood near 'Luke's experimental structure long deserted'. There were some tables scattered about, some with screens round them littered with radio equipment. Metal tubing and teacups were carelessly mingled on others. It all looked remarkably haphazard, untidy and unscientific.

When Lewis went down to Barford for the first test, the apparent inactivity had given place to hectic business. Men were trooping in and out of the hangar; in the middle of it 'as though it were a sacred stone' the white-walled pile stood, a man on top of it, while the wire belonging to some electrical instrument was being disentangled on the floor. As Luke put it, 'we're in the hell of a mess', but the atmosphere was happy, excited, nervous. As they all waited for the trouble with the switch on the control rods to be put right, Lewis noticed the tools of her trade in front of

Mary Pearson, instruments which she must read, a Geiger counter ticking away, two amplifiers of different kinds.

That test was unsuccessful. By the time success at last came in September Barford had gained a new building containing a syphoning plant for heavy water. When Lewis went down there at Martin's request, he was struck by the silence of the hangar in which the pile stood and he did not like it, referring to the 'curious sinister emptiness of the place'. On this visit he went into the Control Room, 'a cubby hole full of shining valves with one kitchen chair placed, domestic and incongruous, in front of a panel of indicators'.

The next addition to Barford was Luke's 'hot' laboratory 'rather like a giant caricature of a school lab'. The work done here was dangerous and there were bells in each section to ring if help were needed. Later still Lewis was taken through a steel door into 'a slit of a room' which was empty except for a safe containing the plutonium.

So from its earliest beginnings as a half-ruined hangar on a deserted field, with a house some way away providing accommodation for the Supervisor and the office staff, Barford developed slowly and little by little into an efficient scientific establishment of which its workers could well feel proud.

Work began in a very small way at Barford in 1941, with Drawbell as Supervisor. Martin joined the staff of mainly refugee scientists in June and Luke came some months later. Many scientists such as Getliffe, had very little belief that the work to be done there would ever lead to anything worthwhile; the Minister himself, Sir Thomas Bevill, did not bother to go and inspect the place personally but sent Lewis instead.

Two main lines of research had been begun — one, under Rudd, the second in command, was to separate the isotope and various methods were being tried, of one of which Martin was at first in charge. The other, under Luke, 'aimed at plutonium'. Martin, himself, was not over-confident in the possibility of success in his particular field; if it came at all it would not be for years. In a difficult interview with Drawbell, Lewis promised to provide him with as many more scientists as possible who would work in both sections.

The next step was Luke's idea that the Canadians might be persuaded to set up a heavy water plant. Sir Hector Rose, the Permanent Secretary, had a different idea; he wanted to close down Barford and send the workers there to join the American research team. While these proposals were under consideration, Martin suddenly forsook Rudd's team for Luke's, in which he had far more faith. He believed that either everybody should concentrate on the manufacture of plutonium, or else that Barford should close down. Sir Thomas Bevill, the Minister, against his personal interests, used his influence, and convinced Sir Hector Rose that Luke's team ought to be supported.

The long slow process of building Luke's 'pile' began. The first instalment of heavy water arrived from Canada. Most of the scientists previously working for Rudd had gone to the USA, to join the researchers there. In fact a race was now in progress. On 22 March everything was at last ready for the first test. If all went well 'the pile would change minute amounts of uranium into plutonium'. All did not go well. First one of the control switches would not work and the test had to be postponed for twenty-four hours. When, in an atmosphere of almost unbearable suspense, it was at last carried out, it was a complete failure. Luke and Martin in their different ways, were heart-broken. Luke argued that if he'd made the whole thing 50% bigger it would have been bound to work. There was much discussion about what had gone wrong. In the end Luke perceived that the uranium had not been pure enough, an impurity called gadolinium must be at the root of the trouble.

The whole thing had to be begun all over again. The scientists managed to jeer at themselves and their expensive non-event. Months passed, secrets were leaked, tension mounted. A syphoning plant for the heavy water was built and on the night of 27-28 September, 1944 the pile began to run. This time Martin had given the test no publicity, but he phoned Lewis when he knew it was a success and his brother went down to Barford immediately.

There was still a long wait ahead. The pile would take 150-200 days to change the uranium into plutonium. The slugs could then be taken out to cool and 90 days after that Luke and Martin could begin to extract the plutonium. Nobody had previously worked with plutonium and they knew it might possess qualities which would be dangerous to the scientists. Though Sawbridge and Martin volunteered, Luke insisted on putting his own hands "inside the blasted stew" and risking the consequences. Both he and Sawbridge became seriously ill, the former critically. Sawbridge had carried Luke away from the rods and rung the bell for help in time for them to be rescued. But there was no thought of giving up the work. Ill as he was, Luke insisted that by the end of June they must start again, adding in a whisper 'we must have more bods'.

New laboratories were being built at Barford when Pearson arrived from America with the news that they had made several bombs over there and were about to test one in the desert. The next news was of the dropping of a bomb on Hiroshima. In spite of the Americans' success, Luke still considered it essential for the British research to go on. Soon all the major nations would be piling up bombs and England could not be left behind. If the number of workers at Barford was doubled he reckoned he might have the bomb in two or three years. Martin, who was offered the post which would once have been his heart's desire, of Supervisor of the establishment, felt unable on conscientious grounds, to accept it, now that the bomb was to be used no longer as a deterrent but as an unbelievably frightful weapon of destruction, aimed at innocent non-combatants; though he stayed long enough to play a leading part in obtaining a confession of espionage from Sawbridge. There was no one else but Luke, in spite of his damaged health, who could take over, and he asked for Rudd as his second-in-command.

The last we are shown of Barford are the two piles already working, under a tall chimney to the accompaniment of the whirring of fans. 'This was Luke's empire, and as he looked over it he thought of nothing but how best to make it run'.

SUMMING-UP

You will have found in this section some widely differing questions including the 'question and answer' type on the *Morte d'Arthur*, straightforward accounts, largely though never entirely a matter of good memory, and the more testing question on *Northanger Abbey*, which calls for careful selection of material scattered throughout the whole novel, rather than concentrating on a comparatively short poem or single scene from a play. By the time you have reached this last section of the book, you should be sufficiently experienced in tackling questions to grasp immediately the methods which have been used here and be able to deal with other questions which do not fit strictly into any of the categories specifically treated.